"I don't have many days left... The US Government is starving me to death... I haven't had food in my stomach in 23 days... I am slowly slipping away and no one notices."

Khalid Qassim, October 13, 2017

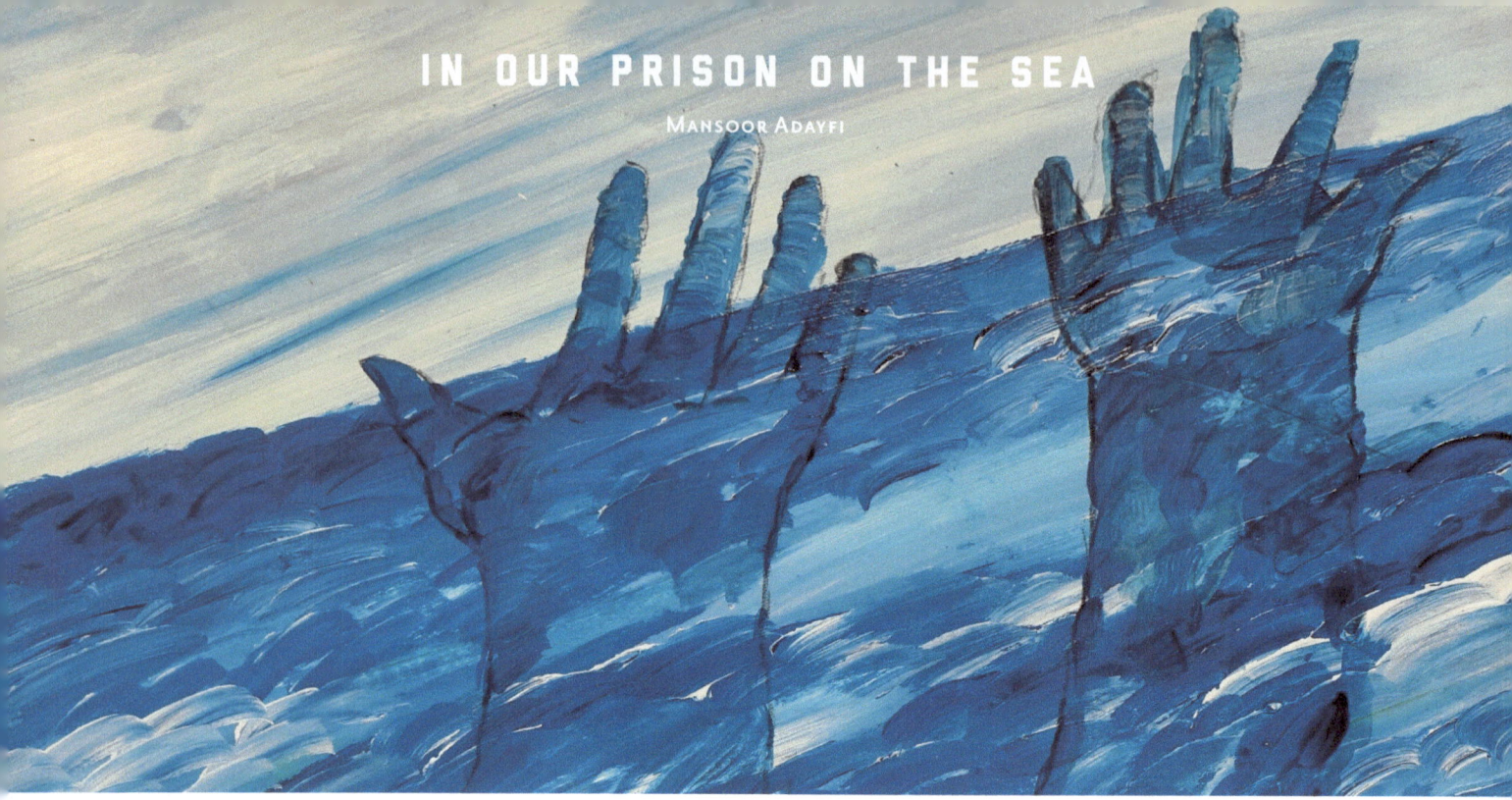

IN OUR PRISON ON THE SEA

Mansoor Adayfi

After the plane landed, a bus took us to a ferry, and beneath it we felt the sea. We were tired, hungry, in pain from beatings along the way, and in fear about it all. We were gagged, blindfolded, and shackled with chains. We were dragged from the ferry to our cages. At our cages, we whispered, There is a sea around. We could feel it despite the marines hitting and kicking us. All we were waiting for at the beginning was the sea.

Few detainees had seen the sea before coming to Guantánamo. All that the Afghans knew was that it was a lot of water that kills and eats people. They started asking about the sea. People who knew what the sea was, mostly people like me, from Arab countries, tried to explain it to the Afghans, but that made them even more afraid.

An Afghan pointed to a cargo plane, and said, "The sea is big like this?"

Bigger, he was told. "Ships can carry many planes that size," another detainee said.

The Afghans told other detainees that the American interrogators threatened them, saying, "When we finish with you here, you will be taken to the sea, and you all will be thrown there."

It wasn't a good beginning with the sea.

When we arrived, the first thing we wanted to know was our location. As Muslims, we pray five times a day, and we must face the Holy Kaaba in Mecca. The direction toward Mecca was impossible to determine when we first got to Guantánamo.

Detainees started to consider the facts available: the weather, the birds, the sea. Then, anything that would tell us about our location. Even dreams. One detainee said, "Based on my dream, we are in Oman." Some guessed we were in India because the pipes that held up our cells' fences had "Made in India" written on them.

Finally, after many months, some detainees who were arrested after

Guantánamo was known about were brought in. They told us we are in Cuba, in Guantánamo. Some of us might have heard of Cuba, but never Guantánamo. Some detainees wouldn't believe it. In the beginning, it was hard for us to pronounce that name, or even memorize it. All we knew was there was the sea.

Some of the camps in Guantánamo were closer to the sea than others. After a few months, we were moved from Camp X-Ray to Camp Delta, which was closer to the sea, but we weren't allowed to see it. The many fences around us were covered with green tarp to block us from seeing the sea. Once, I tried to tear off the tarp, but guards saw me and I was sent to isolation. We tried many times to tear off that tarp. When we did, we saw that there were more walls of fences and tarps, so it was useless.

People will do anything to take their minds away from hell. To remind themselves that a world beyond the hell of Guantánamo still existed, we wanted to show the Afghans the sea. No matter how we described the sea for them, we knew they must see it for themselves. We got some magazines to show them what it looked like. "A lot of water," they said. "How can it carry those ships?" We explained to them about earth and the proportion of the land to the seas, the rivers, the oceans, how ships sail on water and what kind of ships.

Years passed, and we missed everything in our lives.

It was hard not seeing the sea, despite its being only a few hundred feet away from us. At the recreation area, if we lay on our stomach, we could get glimpses of the sea through small openings below the tarp. When the guards found out, they blocked the openings. In some cells, in some blocks, we could stand on the windows at the back of our cells to see the sea, but that was risky, because the guards punished us every time they saw us standing and looking out. Whenever any of us wanted to look at the sea, we needed to ask one of the other detainees to watch for the guards and warn us if they came around

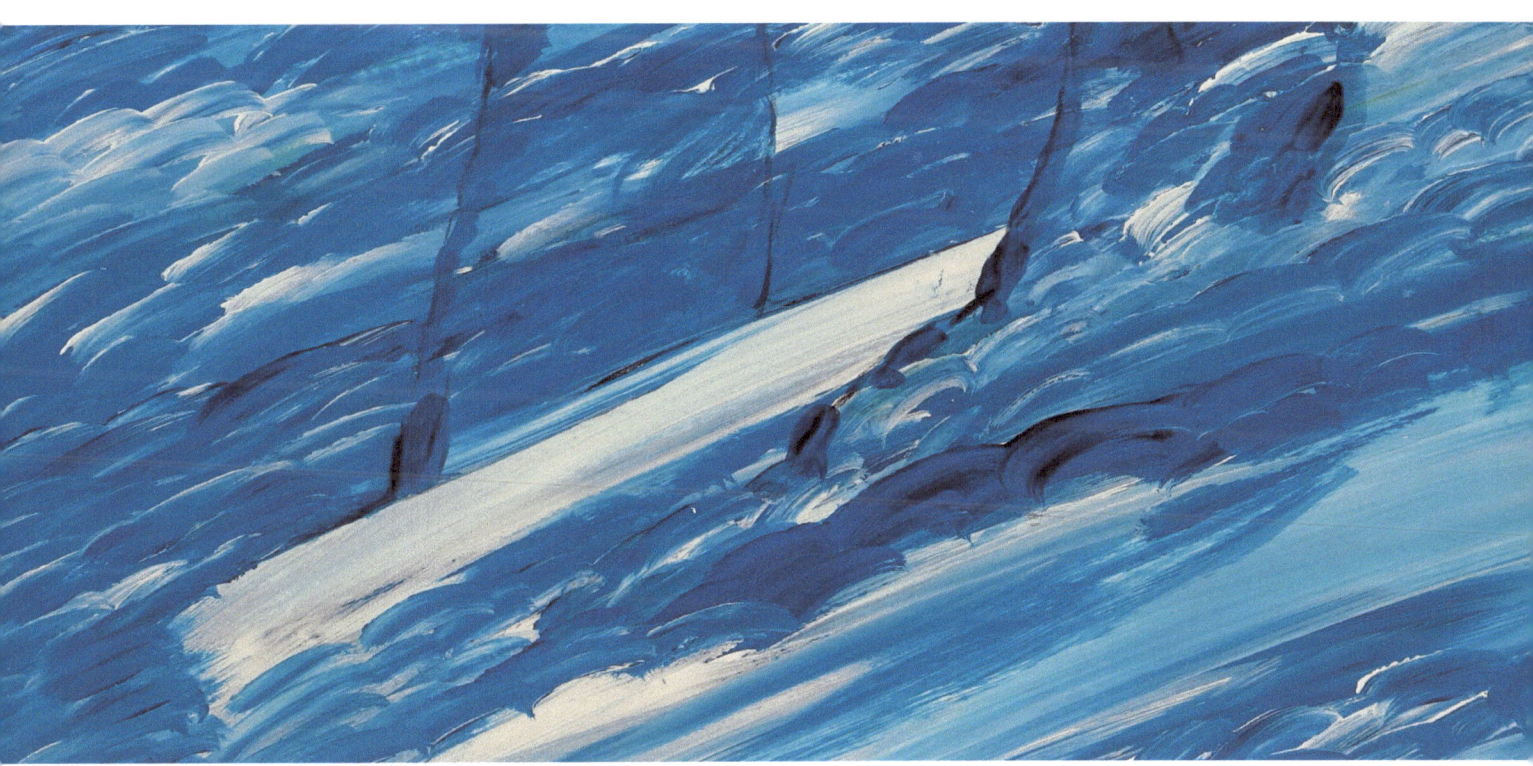

the block. It wasn't long before the administration made higher covers, blocking us from seeing the sea. When we asked why, we were told it was for security and safety.

We couldn't see more than 30 feet beyond our cells at best — walls, fences, green tarps covering everything. I remember how those who couldn't see the sea kept asking the others to tell them what they saw.

But something happened in 2014 that let most of us, finally, see the sea. News that a hurricane was headed toward Cuba caused camp administration to take down the green tarps that blocked us from seeing the sea. The detainees looked so happy when the guards started taking down the covers.

We all faced one direction: toward the sea. It felt like a little freedom, to look at it. I heard an Afghan guy shout, "Allahu akbar!" at the sight, thanking God for the wonder of the sea, repeating that many times, calling out to his friends. The tarps remained down for a few days, and the detainees started making art about the sea. Some wrote poems about it. And everyone who could draw drew the sea. I could see different meanings in each drawing, color and shape. I could see the detainees put their dreams, feelings, hopes and lives in them. I could see some of these drawings were mixtures of hope and pain. That the sea means freedom no one can control or own,

freedom for everyone.

Each of us found a way to escape to the sea.

Those who could see the sea spent most of their time watching, listening and looking at that big blue color, which cools our souls. The sea was a little rough, because of the windy weather. Huge waves that rose high and hit the land. Looking at a sea like that was scary, but it was what we got, and it felt good. Afghans started calling out to one another and expressing their feelings about what they saw, and turned to us with many questions about that beast.

Those days without the tarps were like a vacation. On the last day the sea looked refreshed, calm and lovely. A huge ship sailed close by. Detainees called out to one another to look at the ship. We kept looking at it like something magic would happen and all of us would be freed. But the ship just disappeared. The next day the workers returned and blocked our sight.

Please, enjoy these drawings. Listen to what they tell you. You may think that they are silent, but they are not. They whisper to you in a language you can understand with your feelings. Most of these drawings took months to be completed and months to get approved. They were searched, scanned, and detained. Like us. These drawings had a long, hard journey to get to you. To meet you. Let the sea remind you we are human.

Mansoor Adayfi was held at Guantánamo Bay for 14 years before his transfer to Serbia in July 2016. He is working on a book about his detention. This essay, written for the exhibit and edited by Charles Shields, first appeared in The New York Times on September 15, 2017.

CONTENTS

IN OUR PRISON ON THE SEA — Mansoor Adayfi — 2

POETRY

ODE TO THE SEA — Ibrahim Al-Rubaish — 7

SECOND LANGUAGE — Jericho Brown — 8

I COULD TELL YOU BUT THEN YOU WOULD HAVE TO DESTROY ME — Trevor Paglen — 9

from REACHING GUANTANAMO — Solmaz Sharif — 15

OBEDIENCE — Charles Shields — 18

MONUMENT — Natasha Trethewey — 20

حركة السكوت (NO SPEECH) — Thoom (Zeynab Ghandour) — 21

PROSE

ART THERAPY — Paige Laino — 23

INTERVIEW

Aliya Hana Hussain, Center for Constitutional Rights (CCR); Djamel Ameziane (former detainee and CCR client); Alka Pradhan, Human Rights Counsel at the Guantánamo Bay Military Commissions and formerly Reprieve US; Shelby Sullivan-Bennis, Reprieve US; conducted and edited by Erin Thompson, July 2017 — 27

ARTMAKING AT GUANTANAMO

MOATH AL-ALWI — 33

UNTITLED, WITH MANSOOR ADAYFI — Mala Productions — 35

ARTIST PROFILES

ABDUALMALIK ABUD — 37

AMMAR AL-BALUCHI — 38

AHMED RABBANI — 39

DJAMEL AMEZIANE — 40

GHALEB AL-BIHANI — 41

KHALID QASAM — 46

MOATH AL-ALWI — 48

MUHAMMAD ANSI — 50

letter from MUHAMMAD — 57

MASTHEAD

POETRY

ODE TO THE SEA

Ibrahim al-Rubaish

O sea, give me news of my loved ones.

Were it not for the chains of the faithless, I would have dived into you,
And reached my beloved family, or perished in your arms.

Your beaches are sadness, captivity, pain, and injustice.
Your bitterness eats away at my patience.

Your calm is like death, your sweeping waves are strange.
The silence that rises up from you holds treachery in its fold.

Your stillness will kill the captain if it persists,
And the navigator will drown in your waves.

Gentle, deaf, mute, ignoring, angrily storming,
You carry graves.

If the wind enrages you, your injustice is obvious.
If the wind silences you, there is just the ebb and flow.

O sea, do our chains offend you?
It is only under compulsion that we daily come and go.

Do you know our sins?
Do you understand we were cast into this gloom?

O sea, you taunt us in our captivity.
You have colluded with our enemies and you cruelly guard us.

Don't the rocks tell you of the crimes committed in their midst?
Doesn't Cuba, the vanquished, translate its stories for you?

You have been beside us for three years, and what have you gained?
Boats of poetry on the sea; a buried flame in a burning heart.

The poet's words are the font of our power;
His verse is the salve for our pained hearts.

SECOND LANGUAGE

Jericho Brown

You come with a little
Black string tied
Around your tongue,
Knotted to remind
Where you came from
And why you left
Behind photographs
Of people whose
Names need no
Pronouncing. How
Do you say God
Now that the night
Rises sooner? How
Dare you wake to work
Before any alarm?
I am the man asking,
The great grandson
Made so by the dead
Tenant farmers promised
A plot of land to hew.
They thought they could
Own the dirt they were
Bound to. In that part
Of the country, a knot
Is something you
Get after getting knocked
Down, and story means
Lie. In your part
Of the country, class
Means school, this room
Where we practice
Words like rope in our
Hope to undo your
Tongue, so you can tell
A lie or break a promise
Or grow like a story.

I COULD TELL YOU BUT THEN YOU WOULD HAVE TO DESTROY ME

Trevor Paglen

To be detained at Guantánamo is to be dehumanized. Creating artwork is one of the few means for detainees to fight this dehumanization, by expressing emotions and a love of beauty. Interviews and autobiographical writings show that the military personnel at Guantánamo also feel alienated from normal life – from their family and friends. The secrecy that lies over Guantánamo changes guards and guarded alike.

Like the detainee artists in this exhibit, military personnel have also sometimes allowed the urge for self-expression to overcome some of the restrictions imposed upon them. The artist and scholar Trevor Paglen has examined one example of this phenomenon by cataloguing patches designed and worn by military personnel working on classified missions. These patches, like the detainees' artwork, exist in an uncomfortable space between a desire to broadcast an experience and the need to conceal it. The following is an excerpt from Paglen's book on this project, I Could Tell You But Then You Would Have to Be Destroyed By Me: Emblems from the Pentagon's Black World *(Melville House, 2010).*

To wear an insignia is to tell the world that one is a part of something larger than oneself. In the case of a black unit, wearing insignias that identify oneself as a part of a black unit may actually help to preserve whatever secrets the unit may (or may not) hold. By wearing a patch, its wearer advertises to others around him or her that there are certain things that he or she cannot speak about. His or her membership in the secret society is contingent upon keeping those secrets. We might imagine that wearing a patch that speaks to secrets might be extra incentive for the person wearing the patch to keep silent.

Without a doubt, many members of the black unit are proud of the secrets they hold, and of the clandestine work they've done in the military or intelligence industries. But others struggle with the alienation that comes along with not being able to tell friends and family what one does for a living and with having a secret life. Obtaining and maintaining a security clearance for black projects can involve federal investigators combing through one's personal life, uncomfortable polygraph examinations, and even surveillance.

IF I TELL YOU I HAVE TO KILL YOU (P. 12)

A generic patch for "black" projects designed by a member of Air Test and Evaluation Squadron Four (VX-4), based at Point Mugu near Camarillo, California. VX-4 eventually merged with VX-5 from NAWC China Lake, also in Southern California, to become VX-9 with detachments at both locations.

SEMPER EN OBSCURUS (P. 13)

This patch comes from the Special Projects Office, which operated out of the Air Force's Sacramento Air Logistics Center and oversaw maintenance and support of the F-117A stealth fighter program. The phrase "Semper en Obscurus" translates as "Always in the Dark." The mushroom – which graws in darkness – symbolizes the secret nature of the Office's work. This same patch is now used by the 412th Test Wing's Special Projects Office at Edwards Air Force Base.

ALIEN TECHNOLOGY EXPLOITATION DIVISION (P. 14)

The Alien Technology Exploitation Division patch was designed by Robert Fabian during the time he was assigned to a classified unit working in a security facility at Air Force Space command:

I designed this patch several years ago while stationed at Headquarters, Air Force Space Command. A couple of friends and I pooled our money and had then made – strictly unofficially. I'm afraid there's not a whole lot of symbolism in it. We were working inside a SCIF (vault) and our friends and coworkers used to like giving us a hard time about it, asking if our office was where they kept the alien bodies. As a joke, we told them that dead aliens were no use; we needed live ones to explain their technology to us. After one particularly grueling late night working on briefing slides that went nowhere, we came up with the patch idea. The Klingon translates to "Don't Ask!" We wore them on our flightsuits for a couple of months before anyone in authority spotted them. Our boss's boss's boss, a Brigadier General, only reaction was to ask where he could get one.

A LIFETIME OF SILENCE BEHIND THE GREEN DOOR (P. 15)

The origins and meaning of the patch are obscure. The green figure holding the sword wears the clock-and-dagger garb often associated with black projects. There is a white star in the northern hemisphere (under the letter "S") and a red star in the American Southwest.

The patch is likely associated with the Air Force Intelligence, Surveillance and Reconnaissance Agency, based at Lackland Air Force Base in San Antonio, Texas, which perhawps explains the location of the red star. The Air Force ISR Agency's mission is to "Organize, train, equip, and present assigned forces and capabilities to conduct intelligence, surveillance and reconnaissance for combatant commanders and the nation." The agency is involved in a number of "black" projects. The white star in the sky most likely refers to projects involving space capabilities and systems.

The words "A Lifetime of Silence" no doubt refer to the fact that members of this unit or project cannot speak about what they do. Military intelligence officers have a tradition of working behind locked green vault doors, but the symbol is also widely used in popular culture to designate an inaccessible place.

In Mary E. Wilkins-Freeman's 1917 novel The Green Door, a young girl named Letitia longs to open a mysterious little green door in her house, but her aunt forbids it with the words "It is not best for you, my dear." The 1956 hit song "Green Door" is about a man who couldn't get into a party raging behind a green door. The 1972 pornographic film Behind the Green Door" also uses the image to connote an inaccessible pace (in the case of the film, a sex theater).

IF I TELL YOU I HAVE TO KILL YOU

Trevor Paglen

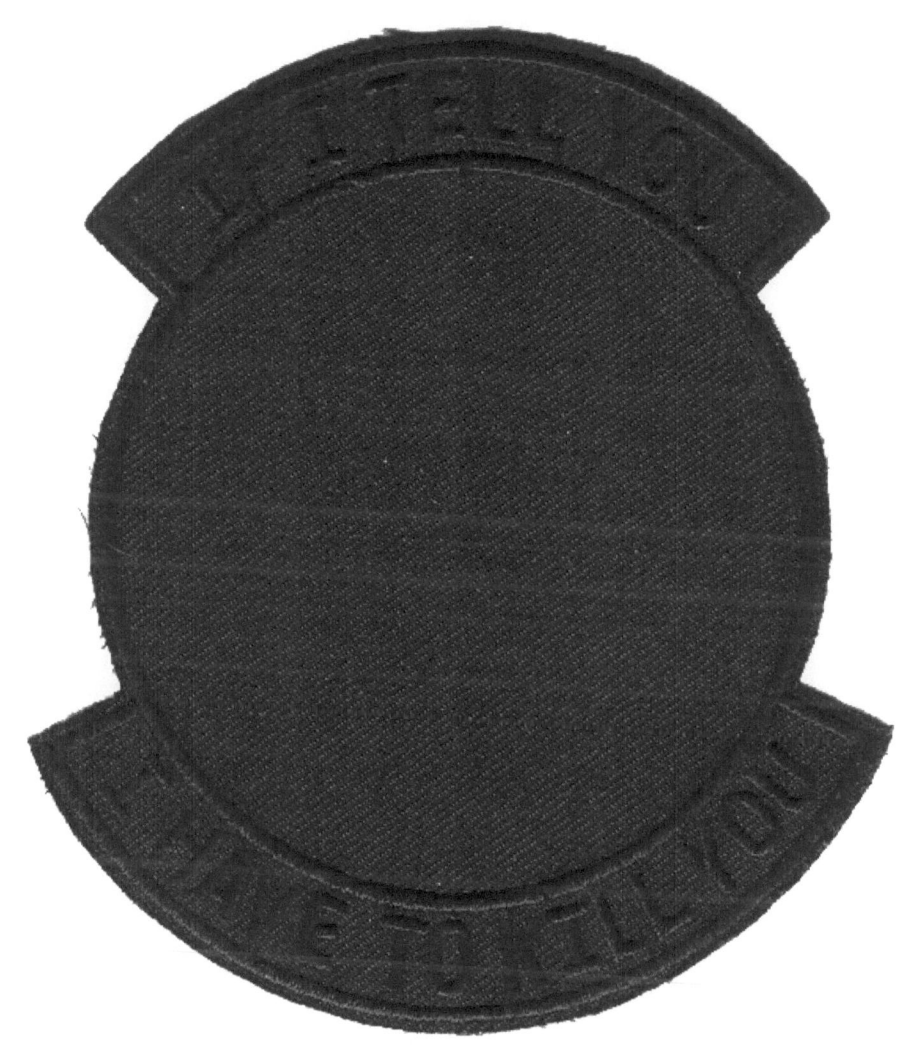

SEMPER EN OBSCURAS

Trevor Paglen

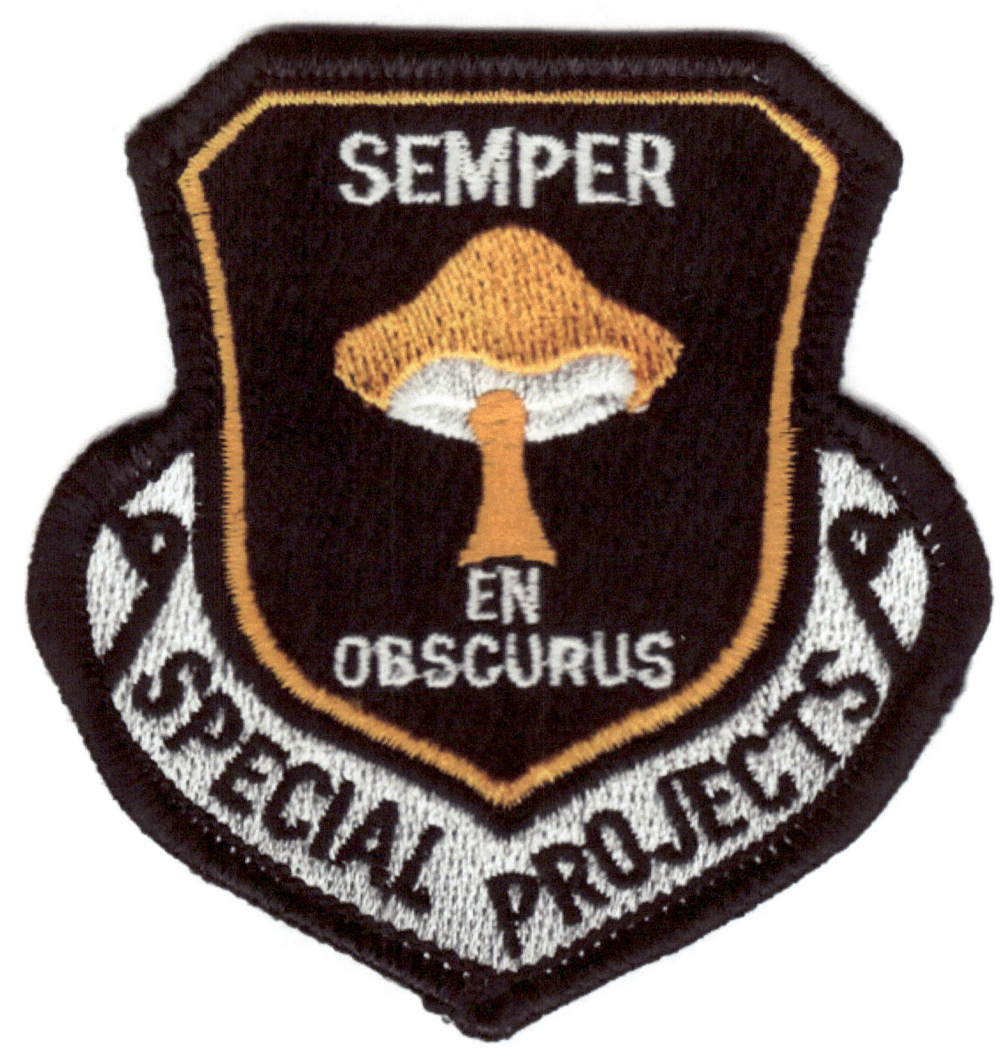

ALIEN TECHNOLOGY EXPLOITATION DIVISION

Trevor Paglen

A LIFETIME OF SILENCE BEHIND THE GREEN DOOR

Trevor Paglen

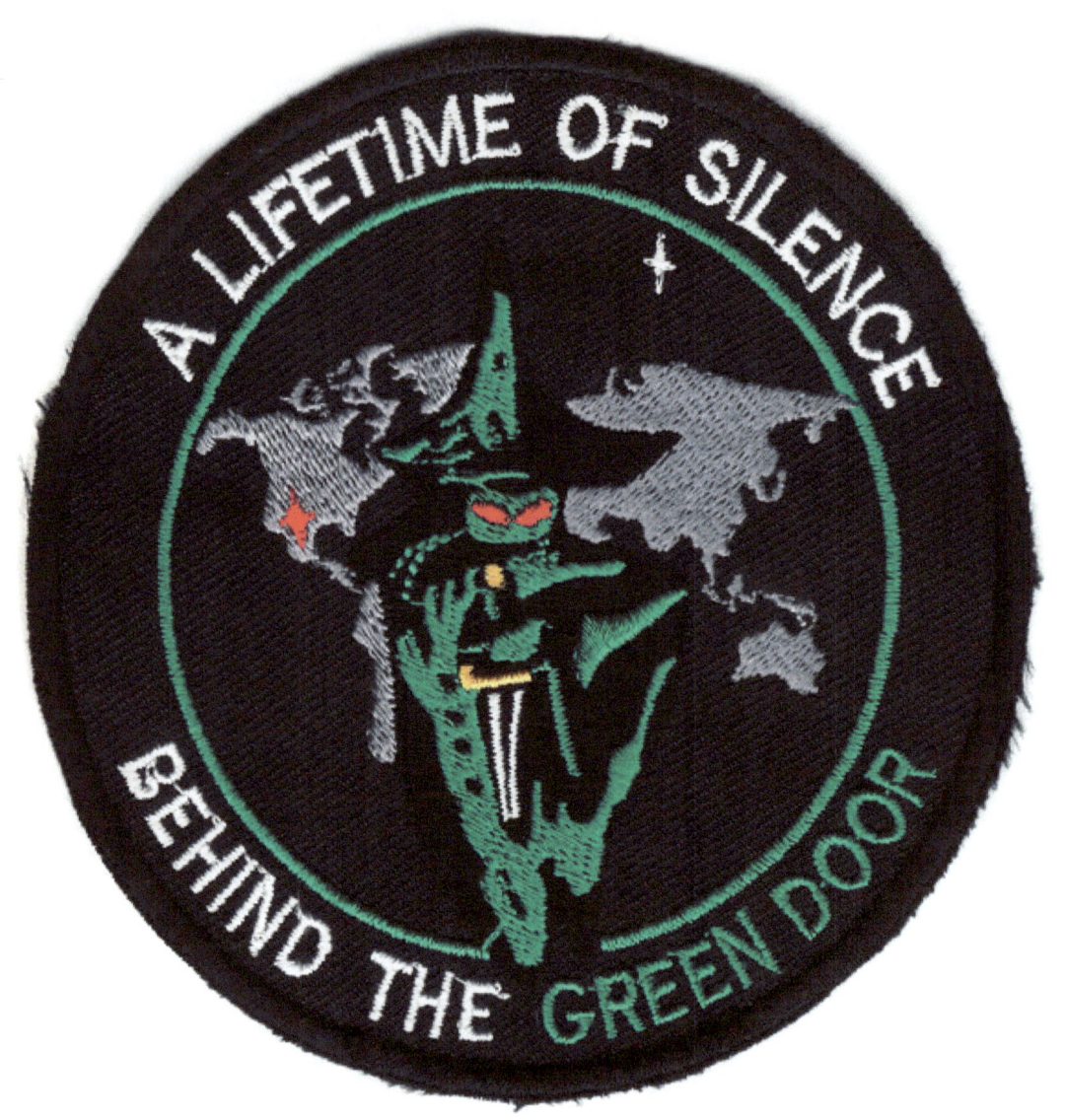

from REACHING GUANTANAMO

Solmaz Sharif

Dear Salim,

At the store, they brought
           already, bruised on the
but still juicy. I pitted sour
           all day, the newspaper
went   with their juice. I save you
jars of preserves for your return.
           some plums, too. I haven't opened
a   since they
         you. Can't stand all those
    , all those   teeth. Or maybe
the   , how they stain upholstery like
    . I hope I don't make you   me
I hope they allow you some   .

Yours

from REACHING GUANTANAMO

Solmaz Sharif

Dear Salim,

have made a nest
under our   . And now
the nestlings always

.
The   of eggs has gone   .
And rice. And tea. I don't know who
decides   things.

Yours,

from REACHING GUANTANAMO

Dear Salim,

The neighbors got an apology
                    and a few thousand dollars.
They calculate   based on
            and
and age. The worth of a   , of a human
            .   hands shook as she opened
                    . She took it out front
and ripped it   .   a little pile
and set fire to it right there, right in front of

            .
        says they'll send me
a check   for   . I would
            !   !
            ? Never.

Yours,

OBEDIENCE

for Mansoor Adayfi

CHARLES SHIELDS

I

And so it was. And so I will
turn like a planet towards the rain.
            Render my life tiny enough to detain
the future it recalls. I will stare
        at the sea
                of a nation's faith refraining it ain't
        native to splitting its story's skull
    open like a water-
            melon of suicide last Tuesday. I can almost taste
                        the circumference of faith in relation
                to the punishment of surrender it holds
                            together
                    like plastic threaded with gold.
                            One glint
                in which fear defiles beauty
                    by dying for it,
        a white god says, gazing endlessly
                        at everything
            but what's there. I'm an artist
    because I stare. I feel it in my black hair
    blooming bigger than the trace of mistaken words
a prison god sang against it;
    as if we gave words nothing. But I know you
                    gave them everything.

II

Enter the room you paid for,
he says. Enter never.
Don't be afraid. Space
will never be emptier
than the windows we are born
to share. I lug
the space my life bears up and run down
a powerless mountain of sorrow
with my mouth open because I love
to taste the air
and feel like I'm going somewhere
as the smell of the ink of my ancestors fades beneath
the seasons of bleach it survived.
Enter that room,
the man I once thought a god whispers again, so softly
I know he's not alive.
I close my eyes. I close my eyes. Enter
the room, a dead god says.
Father, I say,
as my eyes adjust to the dark. Father,
we never left.

MONUMENT

Natasha Trethewey

Today the ants are busy
  beside my front steps, weaving
in and out of the hill they're building.
  I watch them emerge and —

like everything I've forgotten — disappear
  into the subterranean — a world
made by displacement. In the cemetery
  last June, I circled, lost —

weeds and grass grown up all around —
  the landscape blurred and waving.
At my mother's grave, ants streamed in
  and out like arteries, a tiny hill rising

above her untended plot. Bit by bit,
  red dirt piled up, spread
like a rash on the grass; I watched a long time
  the ants' determined work,

how they brought up soil
  of which she will be part,
and piled it before me. Believe me when I say
  I've tried not to begrudge them

their industry, this reminder of what
  I haven't done. Even now,
the mound is a blister on my heart,
  a red and humming swarm.

حركت السكوت (NO SPEECH)

Thoom (Zeynab Ghandour)_

PROSE

ART THERAPY

Paige Laino

The American Art Therapy Association states "creating art and reflecting on the art products and processes can increase awareness of the self and cope with symptoms of stress and traumatic experiences." The Association is, of course, referring to artmaking under the direction of an accredited Art Therapist, but the statement seems broadly applicable. The few public mentions of an art instructor for detainees held at Guantánamo refer only to a Jordanian man known simply as "Adam," and who could be reasonably assumed to have no such training, but there is no doubt the artmaking process is, for detainees, therapeutic.

"For the most part, anyone can use art therapy," the Association continues. That truly does mean anyone – be it those held in indefinite detention without charge, or those who initiated the mechanisms to hold them.

Former President George W. Bush does not have a CV, or at least not one accessible without submitting a FOIA request, but since his first paintings were leaked in 2013, he has had two solo exhibitions at his own presidential library and was included in a group show at the "Freedom Conference and Festival." His first monograph was released in February of 2017, in which he writes that he found painting because he

"was antsy." He continues, "My life didn't seem complete. I wanted a new adventure—within the confines of the post-presidential bubble."

Portraits of Courage: A Commander in Chief's Tribute to America's Warriors is, basically, exactly that: it is a book of portraits of and inspirational anecdotes about veterans wounded in the Iraq and Afghanistan wars. In the tantalizingly terse introduction by Bush, which could itself begin a thousand more essays, he says he "painted these men and women as a way to honor their service to the country and show my respect for their sacrifice and courage."

The artwork in this exhibition finds an almost too-easy foil in the artwork made by George W. Bush. Most obviously, both of these bodies of work would not exist without conflict initiated by the president-turned-painter. Bush frames the subjects of his portraits as those who were wounded while "[volunteering to] defend our country." In the same light, detainees were benevolently permitted to create art while their threat level to homeland security is still being investigated. According to this narrative, neither these wounded warriors nor these indefinite detainees are still reeling from the ramifications of the wars in Iraq and Afghanistan, nor the Authorization for Use of Military Force Against Terrorists, all of which were enacted by Bush.

The Art Therapy Association again describes the uniqueness of artmaking: "most other forms of communication elicit the use of words or language. Often times, humans are incapable of expressing themselves within this limited range." In the former President's case, the limitation

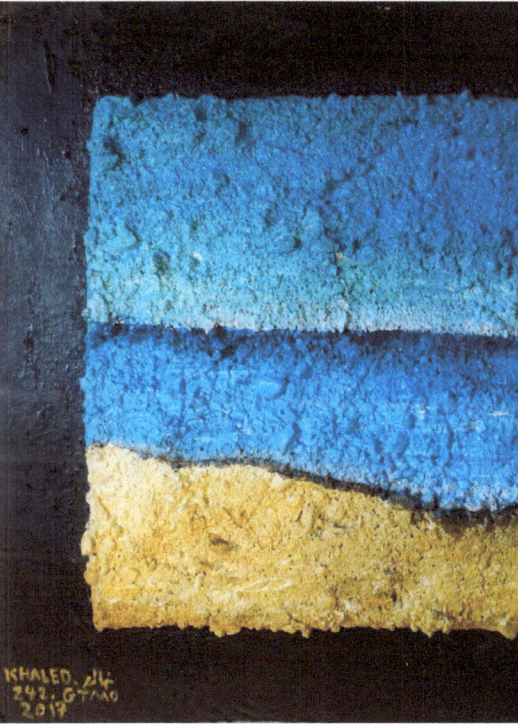

of his expression appears to be self-imposed by his ill-defined 'bubble.' For detainees who are encouraged to communicate with guards and staff only through intermittently available interpreters because their grasp of English has led to perilous miscommunication, art is the best way for them to express complex emotions with the fewest barriers..

In the still-limited avenues for contact available to them in the lead up to this show, The detainees have been quite frank about what they want their work to communicate. While some detainees use artwork in a more overtly healing way — for instance, Ammar's piece visualizing

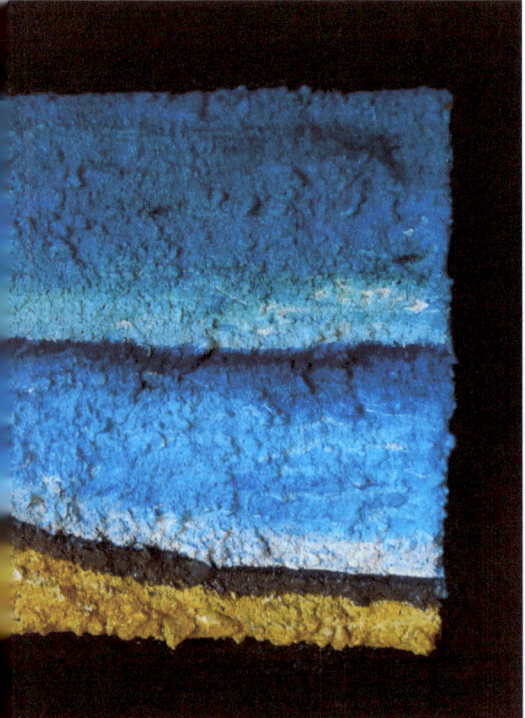

the vertigo he has suffered since being repeatedly tortured during countless interrogations — others hope that their work simply humanizes them to viewers.

"I want people to think we are not negative people.... We only make beautiful things. We love life, we love everything and people. We are not extremists, we

do not hate nice things. I want [an American audience] to think about us in this way," said Moath al-Alwi.

"For many years we Guantanamo prisoners were pictured by many US government officials as monsters, the evilest people on earth, the worst of the worst, and I am sure many Americans believed that. Displaying the artwork is a way to show people that we are people who have feelings, who are creative, that we are human beings. We are normal people and not monsters," Djamel Ameziane wrote through his lawyer.

As mentioned elsewhere, information about the conditions under which detainees made art at Guantanamo is scarce. Despite that fact, we can say much more about how the detainees used artwork to express themselves therapeutically than we can from reading all 191 pages written by George W. Bush about what, exactly, he intends to work through in his portraits of veterans.

Though his introduction does a shockingly skillful job of shifting any accountability for the wars in which these people fought away from himself, and the various accounts of redemption and recovery are about the veterans rather than himself, one could generously read this book as a tome of atonement. While he claims to have come up with the idea of painting Iraq and Afghanistan war veterans at the gentile prompting of a friend to broaden his repertoire beyond world leaders, it is hard to not interpret his

98 portraits, "each done with a lot of care and respect," as an act of penance.

These portraits were all done from photographs. The former president vaguely suggests that he met these veterans on charity tours, and his anecdotes all seem very personal, but he still chooses to paint from static images rather than embarking on the task of having his subjects sit with him. The referents are distant.

The referents are distant for artists at Guantanamo Bay as well. From what we know, even the most basic still life included in this exhibition is painted from a photograph, either printed from the internet or scanned from a book. Despite the many landscapes, there is no plen air in the camp, and instead detainees generate whole worlds from the trickle of National Geographics, VHSes, and bootlegged satellite news channels accessible to them.

The detainees take images of places they've never been and activate them with their caged imagination. An almost perfect inverse, George W. Bush's world leader series was proven to be painted from the top Google Image Search results for each world leader; he, in a unique position to have seen these important figures in intimate settings, reduced their personage to mildly stylized photorealism.

When images of his first paintings were leaked in 2013, at a time when Bush was already faint in the age of Obama, his foray into the artworld was met with the same gentile derision that marked most of his presidency. In an age where "Buck Fush" bumper stickers have been covered by "Hope," "Love Trumps Hate," then "Not My President," it is easy to forget the bizarre space he occupied in the American consciousness while he was actually in office. Even at his worst, he was seen as an at most accidental abettor to war crimes: in an uncomfortably relevant relic of the recent past, "Harold and Kumar Escape from Guantanamo Bay," released in 2008, George W. Bush acts as the last minute savior to the duo. He is both comically aware of the horrific human rights abuses at the camp, but willing to help a "fellow stoner" avoid being baselessly detained at the camp he seemingly unknowingly created.

His artwork, like his military campaigns, seemed to illicit a feeling of, "well, gosh, at least he's trying." It is unsurprising that the artwork of this apparently-lovable scamp has been reviewed by Jerry Saltz, Roberta Smith, Peter Schjeldahl, and many more art critics with actual career-making cultural cache. He remains consummately blameless, and the recipient of good fortune.

The body of artwork in this show, artwork which owes just as much of its creation to the aggression of the Bush administration, and provides a perhaps even more insightful look into the lasting wounds of the War on Terror, has not received as much attention. This is the first exhibition of artwork made by detainees while inside Guantánamo. If an artist who happens to be a war criminal waiting indefinitely to be charged can have two solo shows, we hope these detainees can exhibit more too.

INTERVIEWS

ARTMAKING AT GUANTÁNAMO

Aliya Hana Hussain, Center for Constitutional Rights (CCR); Djamel Ameziane (former detainee and CCR client); Alka Pradhan, Human Rights Counsel at the Guantánamo Bay Military Commissions and formerly Reprieve US; Shelby Sullivan-Bennis, Reprieve US; conducted and edited by Erin Thompson, July 2017

THE EXPERIENCES OF DETAINEES AND LAWYERS VARY GREATLY.

PARTICIPANTS OPINION'S AND PERCEPTIONS OF THE FACTS ARE THEIR OWN, AND NOT NECESSARILY SHARED BY OTHERS.

When did art-making at Guantánamo begin and how was it handled by the authorities?

SSB: They were always allowed some of it for super compliant detainees (i.e., at Camp Iguana in the early days) but the formal teaching of it came in about around 2009. They used to do simple drawings. But that always got censored. In the early days we were told by the secure facility people that the prisoners might put squiggles into their art as messages to al Qaeda…. then we got banned from getting out things because they were embarrassing (Sami el Haj's pictures of forced feeding, etc.). Nothing used to get out. Then a few random birthday cards and so forth began to slip out around 2006 or 2007.

DA: The official art class started in late 2008 or 2009. It was the camp authorities' initiative. Before that, as far as I can remember,

no prisoner was allowed to draw anything, even a flower or a heart

in their letters. Some prisoners used to write to their families; in these cases the drawing was blacked out with a black marker. The same thing happened to the letters sent by the families.

AHH: We've heard stories of detainees making artwork by sketching flowers and such into styrofoam cups in the very early Bush years, and that the guards confiscated those and took them to

be analyzed by intelligence to see if they had coded messages. I bet a lot of artwork from the early days, if it existed at all, were destroyed. I can't imagine detainees being allowed to take it with them when they were released.

When and why did art-making become authorized at Guantánamo?

AP: For the men held at Camp 7 (including my client, Ammar al Baluchi), security is much tighter as the government labels them "high value detainees"—which just means that they were tortured by the CIA in secret prisons abroad. Therefore, art-making has never been explicitly sanctioned, and they have only occasionally been allowed to have access to art supplies such as colored pencils and crayons. Ammar's art pieces are small in number as a result, but each one is deeply meaningful.

SSB: Our clients' earliest work is dated 2011, but we only started to get the artwork released from the prison around 2015.

AHH: Most of Djamel's artwork was made between 2009 and 2011. The first time I saw any public reporting on detainee artwork was a 2010 Slate article, where media visiting the base were given a tour that included an art display. The timing of the art classes and allowing media to take photos of the displays makes sense. Obama was now in the office, and according to the Slate article, it was just around the time journalists were coming to the base to cover the Omar Khadr trial (who was detained at sixteen). Surely artwork at Gitmo helped support the idea that under the new President, Gitmo was a better and more humane place.

Tell us more about the art classes and instructor.

AP: Camp 7 has never been allowed to have art classes or instructors. The men there have been held in close-to **solitary confinement for over ten years,** and are rarely allowed even to speak to each other.

DA: At the beginning there was a Sudanese instructor. He stayed for only about a month and left. We started drawing with charcoal crayon and (wax color) crayon. That wasn't really serious. Then another instructor came: a Jordanian-Iraqi named "Adam." When I left GTMO in late 2013 he was still there. He started with the basics and after a while, we were provided with watercolor paint and brushes. After our repeated requests to the authorities, later we were provided with acrylic paint and plaster carving and other materials, as well as Arabic calligraphy for those of the prisoners who were interested. Personally, I was only interested in painting and drawing.

SSB: I've been told by multiple clients that for the last several months, there has been no art instructor, and that the class is taught by someone with a background in engineering whose job is to teach another course. Some men prefer to only attend class for access to the materials, rather than the instruction, and are proudly self-taught, like Khalid Qasim.

Oddly, I have always heard that there is a lack of art supplies for my clients—not enough paper to draw on, effectively. This is particularly perplexing when you consider the amount of money allocated to keeping the men in prison without charging them—a whopping $10.84 million per year, per client (which, if you were wondering, breaks down

to over $29K per night!). You'd think they could cough up an extra paint brush or two for what the guard force and the detainees mutually agree (for different reasons) is a good use of their time.

What are the rules for making art? How have they changed?

DA: As for the rules, we were only allowed to have the materials given to us by the instructor. We were not allowed to draw or paint anything in connection with , the "camp security" or that sends a political or an ideological message.

AHH: Since 2010, CCR has sent down art materials for our clients, including drawing paper, pastels, acrylics, and "how to" books. During the hunger strike in 2013, there were instances where many of the prisoners' personal possessions were confiscated, and I think this included any art-related materials that they had. Most of the supplies were provided through art class. I suspect that art and other classes were only for the most compliant, those in Camp 6.

SSB: As with all things in GTMO, the rules around art-making change frequently and seemingly arbitrarily: the number of canvases that they're allowed to work on at any given time, the number of pieces they've made that they're allowed to keep in their cell.

But most importantly, what they're allowed to paint changes—or rather, what they paint that gets released from the prison. There was a time when nothing was making its way out of GTMO; now they're allowing a good deal of material out, but only what the government wants being released. **Depictions of suffering** are **more or less** categorically **banned from release.** This is by far the biggest complaint with regard to art that my clients have.

It's quite rare that detainees or counsel are given a reason for the denial of certain pieces' release. Indeed, I've only ever been offered an explanation once, read from a piece of paper that I was denied a copy of. But suffice it to say that of the hundreds of paintings my clients have shown me, in my experience, it is only the abstract spots on white background, and serene depictions of lakes that manage to claw their way out of that place.

What are the sources for the images used by your clients in their art?

AP: Ammar looks at photographs, but also draws from his own imagination. In particular, he draws to exorcise some of the torture effects that he still suffers, as is clear from his "Vertigo" piece. As physical and psychological health care is withheld from the tortured men in Camp 7, this is one of the few methods of self-therapy he has.

DA: The instructor printed pictures from the internet or sometimes he would copy pictures from art books with the copy machine. Also, as source of inspiration, we used pictures from magazines provided by the prison library, like National Geographic.

SSB: I am always asking Ahmed Rabbani where he has seen the incredible village, building, monument, etc. that he has painted and his answer is always to tap his temple and smile. Sometimes he dreams them, sometimes he merges different places he's seen on television over the years—famous sites in countries to which he never had the economic privilege to travel. He spent almost two years in a black site before being brought to Guantánamo and a good deal of what he paints relates back to that time. None of those paintings are released.

Tell us more about how art was/is displayed at Guantánamo.

AP: There is no public display of detainee art, even though there are glamour shots of iguanas in the mess hall that could do with a change! My clients have simply stuck some of their artwork on the walls of their cells, or kept them in folders to show attorneys during visits.

DA: All I know is that our artwork was displayed for the media tours, I think in the prison library.

How does artwork leave Guantánamo, and for what purposes?

AP: Ammar has given us some of his artwork for safekeeping, since we never know when the guards may be ordered to sweep the cells. In the past, they have confiscated all sorts of things, including legal mail, so art is not safe.

AHH: Until approximately 2015, artwork was only able to leave the prison via the International Committee of the Red Cross (ICRC) directly to detainees' families. For example, all of Djamel's artwork was sent to his brother in Canada through the ICRC, and then he would send us photos or originals to our office (even though he wanted to send some of his artwork directly to us). If lawyers were to take any artwork out of the attorney-client meetings before 2015, we would have to submit them to the Privilege Review Team (PRT) and they would be treated like our meeting notes. When our clients brought artwork to meetings, they had not previously been stamped for release by Joint Task Force (JTF), which is why we had to get them "declassified" some other way. Most often, the PRT would not clear that artwork for release (they weren't directly related to their legal case, it was a pain, etc.), so we would usually tell our clients to go through the usual channels of sending their work through the ICRC to their families. I don't really know why the rules changed, and JTF stamped the artwork to be given to lawyers to take out, but it was long overdue. I can only speculate, but beautiful and innocuous artwork of landscapes and flowers helped humanize our clients and the administration in their efforts to clear men through PRBs, and repatriate and resettle cleared guys.

What does making art mean for your clients?

AP: For Ammar, I believe that art is a way to try and express the pain (physical and mental) that comes from having been tortured for over 14 years. He has very real physical ailments—a traumatic brain injury and strained ligaments among others—but also crippling PTSD and anxiety, along with an inability to

sleep as a result of sleep deprivation. When he expresses himself through art or another medium, it allows him to better analyze his issues and explain them to us.

DA: In my case, art work represented a form of expression during my prison time: expression of my feelings about the unclear future; things we were deprived of; things that I dreamed of. I wasn't trying to send any form of message through my artwork.

AHH: For our client Ghaleb Al-Bihani, art was a way that he passed the time at Guantánamo and you can see his skills improve dramatically over a short period of time. He saw himself as part of an artist community, and always welcomed feedback from their public, especially artists, since he knew that CCR used his artwork in our public advocacy. His artwork was a way for him to connect to the outside world. As he once wrote,

"Painting makes me feel as if **I am embracing the universe...** I also see things around me as if they were paintings, which gives me the sense of a beautiful life."

SSB: Ahmed Rabbani, from what other detainees tell me, is widely regarded one of the best artists remaining at GTMO. He takes his art very seriously, is always asking for materials to learn new techniques and also to learn about the works of renowned artists, past and present. As someone who was tortured brutally for an extensive period of time, art is a kind of catharsis for him. Separately from that, in a world where the capacity for personal achievement (and its recognition) is quite hard to find, art is a skill at which he has become very good. It is an opportunity for personal pride amidst a panoply of rules meant to humiliate and degrade. It's everything to him.

Another client of mine, Haroon Gul, takes his art much less seriously—he openly mocks his ability to paint and depict anything recognizable, but he continues to incorporate his

daughter's name

into almost every piece. He has drawn more copies than I can count of a photo that he has of his daughter; in its final iterations, his sketch is the spitting image of the photo. He also uses art as a way to gift me something, as he often says that he feels he has nothing with which he can thank me. He has asked if my mom would want something and what might she like. I told him she likes the ocean, and he somehow managed to find seashells to attach to a piece that bears her name. He uses art to show love.

Why do you think your clients agreed to have their art displayed in this show?

AP: Ammar knows that he and all other men at Guantánamo have been dehumanized to Americans; that they are thought of and portrayed as **monsters**.

That dehumanizing process has been perhaps the worst part of their treatment in U.S. custody. He sees this as an opportunity to show that they are all human beings with the same feelings any of us have.

DA: The reason why I agreed to have my artwork displayed in this show is that, for many years we Guantánamo prisoners were pictured by many US government officials as monsters, the evilest people on earth, the worst of the worst, and I am sure many Americans believed that. Displaying the artwork is a way to show people that we are people who have feelings, who are creative, that **we are human beings.** We are normal people and not monsters.

AHH: I think that our clients have agreed to participate in this exhibit because they have always seen their artwork as an expression of who they are and a way to connect to what was going on outside of the prison. They're unable to come to the U.S. and speak directly to the public, so displaying their artwork is a way that they can share their story directly and (hopefully) be seen as individuals, and as artists. They are also interested in efforts to keep the spotlight on Guantánamo and making sure the public does not forget about Guantánamo, and the 41 men who remain.

SSB: There are various motivations for my clients, but the common purpose—that is also the preeminent purpose—is because they want people to know that they are human, still in Guantánamo, and still suffering. Ahmed Rabbani draws intricate painting after intricate painting depicting luxurious restaurants, buffets, and table settings; he wants to open a restaurant, **he still has that dream** of a life outside GTMO, and he is still stuck on the inside being **denied** any opportunity to defend himself with a trial. Khalid Qasim wants people to understand what GTMO is; he doesn't want Americans to slide into a quiet comfort thinking that the degradation and cruelty ended with the entrance of Obama. He makes art for the same reason that he continues his long-term hunger strike: peaceful resistance as a means to reclaim dignity.

What piece of art made at Guantánamo means the most to you, and why?

AP: I have two that I think I are very special. The first is the piece that Ammar has titled "Vertigo," because it's such a raw depiction of something that I've seen him go through many times, and **it tells me what he sees** when he has to stop talking, stop participating in his capital defense, and close his eyes for a minute. The second is an untitled picture of the beach and the sea, which I find to be deeply sad. Ammar has lived very near the sea at Guantánamo for nearly eleven years after 3.5 years of CIA custody, and has never once laid eyes on it. This piece is solely from his imagination.

DA: The one with a boat out at sea, battered by storm, because it reflected what I was living in prison. We were always badly treated by the guards: **beaten,** provoked, **dragged** on the floor, brutally **pushed**, bodily searched three or four times a day, and they disturbed us when we were sleeping and sometimes deprived us from sleeping for over 24 hours and many other things including psychological torture. All that on a daily basis for years and years. It gave me the impression of being a boat facing storm after storm after storm that seemed to never end.

AHH: There's a painting that Ghaleb Al Bihani made especially for me. It's a beautiful scene: a long path that leads into a body of water, with a small table with two seats next to a tree. First, I was just struck by how selfless this gift was – that he took time to create something for special for me. He made a painting for everyone on this team, and they were all so different and showed that he thought deeply about how to personalize them. I love the river and the water, which for me symbolize hope, the future, and life's potential, and saw the table set for two as a symbol of friendship and the importance of moving through this life with others by your side.

I used to be angry about the JTF stamps on the back of artwork--a way for the prison authorities to have a claim over everything (and everyone) in its custody. But now it serves to remind me of our clients' resistance and resilience, and that beauty can emerge from even the darkest of places. The human spirit knows no bounds. Plus, Ghaleb is a free man now.

INTERVIEW, with MOATH AL-ALWI

GUANTANAMO BAY, CUBA, MAY 15, 2017

Does art help you deal with being at Guantanamo?

In 2009 and 2010, I was so **bored**. There was so much empty time. I thought, how should I spend my time? So I started making art. Art filled that emptiness. I started making things, making progress. I realized this is a way to fill the time, but also to enjoy the time passing by.

Around 2012, **I was in a windowless cell. I thought, how can I open a window in the cell?** I took pictures from magazines – mountains, trees – and put them up in my cell. Then I thought of something else – a watermill. I made a watermill out of small cups and put it in front of the air conditioner, so all day long it was turning. It didn't twirl at first. Then I found a way, using a pen, to control the speed. It took me some time. This is how I started creating things.

Then, I thought of making a model of a window. I drew palm trees, an island, a sea, small boats, a house with windows and doors that opened and closed. It was a large window. The palm trees were in relief. Everyone came to enjoy the work. I lost it. I don't know where it is. But I think it still exists, some brothers said they saw it.... But I have lost hope, I will not get it back.

Now how does art help you cope with being here?

Well, in general, when I start an artwork, I forget I am in prison. I start a little before dawn and I work for seven or eight hours. When I start an artwork, I forget myself.

Even the ship, when I started building it, cutting pieces, I forgot myself. The most beautiful thing was when I was cutting the ropes. I imagined myself on the ship in the middle of the ocean. One day, I was tired, and the ship was on the floor, and a fan blew air into the sails and the ship started moving.

Every day **my brothers help me**. They say, forget about your troubles and problems, just work on the ship.

What materials do you use?

I try to use whatever is available. I try to make it as close to reality. I try to use what is around me because I don't have access to real things. Like the gondola - I wanted to make a seat and I saw the sponge. So I made the seat from the sponge. Sometimes I use plastic material from shampoo bottles, sometimes cartons and cardboard. One of the officers told me, "I hope you remain here so you will become more creative."

Sometimes I just experiment. If I do something wrong, I try a different way to get a better result. My personality means that I don't despair easily. If I fail, I try again and again. Like the ship - the mechanical movement of the helm was very hard to make it, since different materials I tried for the ropes acted differently. I tried and tried and tried until I found that dental floss is strong and smooth and had light friction and could make the helm work. The crow's nests at the tops of the masts were very hard to make. They broke. I tried again and again for an entire day. It was very difficult. Every single detail was difficult.

For the ship's flags, I chose green. Green represents nature and life. I put an eagle's wings as the bowsprit to symbolize freedom. There's a story behind this: once, when I was in Camp 5, I was gazing through a small window and I saw an eagle. I wished I was this eagle. I told my brothers, I wish I had wings.

In the ship's portholes, there are pictures of Jerusalem, Mecca, and Medina. You can't see them unless you look through the portholes.

I didn't have the right material for the anchor. Finally, I found the lid of a spray can and tried, as usual, once or twice until I was able to make it. All these small details.

What would you like people to know or think about when they are looking at your art?

I want people to think we are not negative people, we don't have negative thoughts. We only

make beautiful

things. We love life, we love

everything and people. We are not extremists, we do not hate nice things. I want them to think about us this way.

What are you thinking about when you are creating art?

I think about how to get out of this prison. Despite being in prison, I try as much as I can to get my soul out of prison. I live a different life when I am making art. Every time I finish one piece, I clean my room and start a new work. My prayer rug is stained with paint.

Interview has been condensed and edited by Erin Thompson.

UNTITLED, *with MANSOOR ADAYFI*

EDITED BY MELANEY PORTILLO AND AMANDA KING
MALA PRODUCTIONS

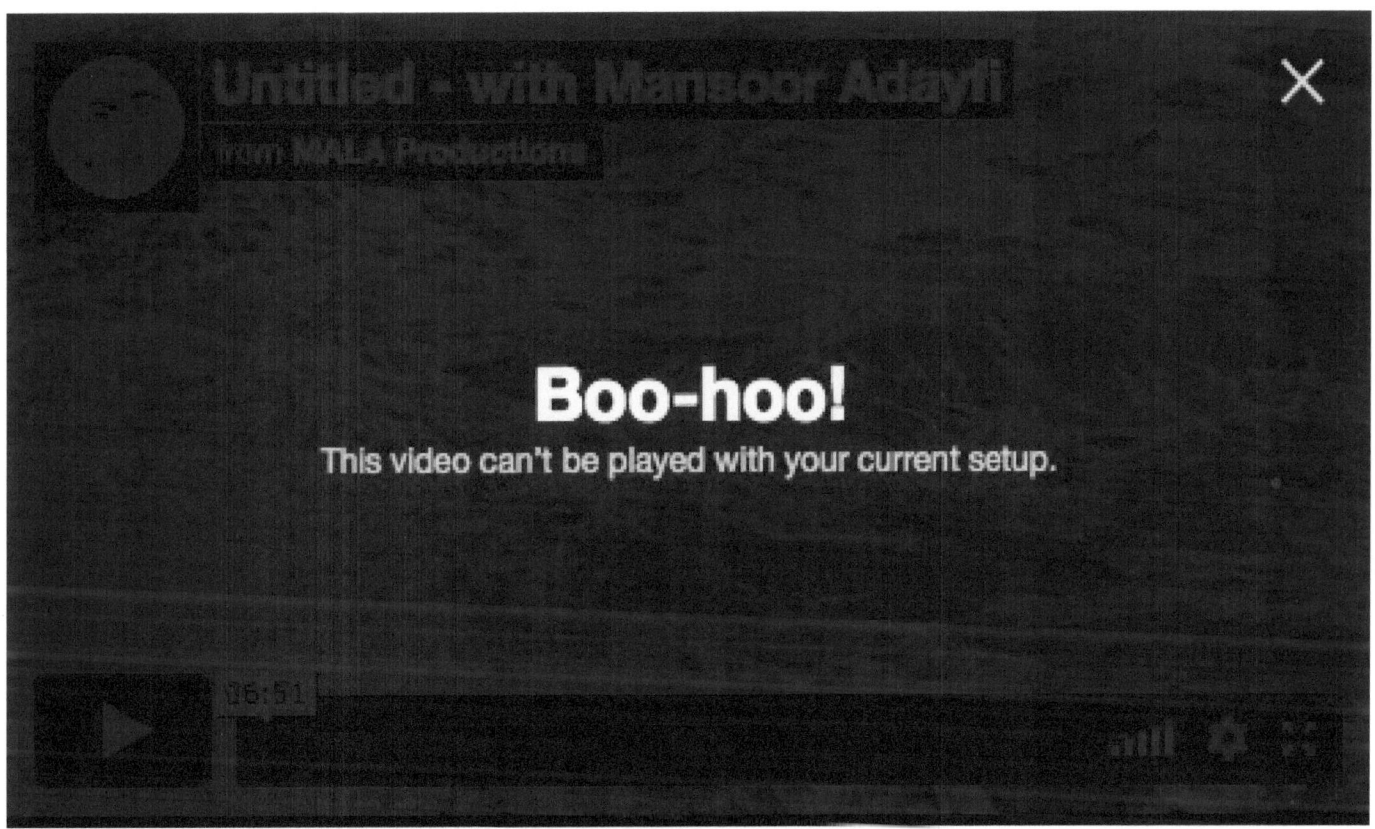

ARTIST PROFILES

ABDUALMALIK ABUD

Abdualmalik (Alrahabi) Abud, originally from Yemen, was detained at Guantánamo for almost 15 years before being released to Montenegro in 2016. He began creating art during his last years at Guantánamo. Whenever he thought of his wife and daughter, he would begin to draw in order to forget that he was imprisoned. He frequently drew the complex architecture of Sana'a, Yemen.

Adbulmalik told curators, "what I want people to know when they look at my art is that we are humans, we have feelings and emotions, we love life, and we are not like they pictured us."

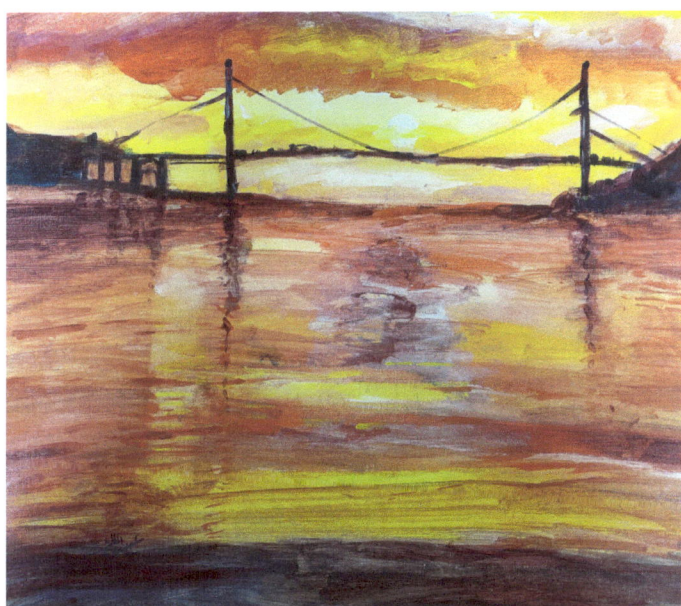

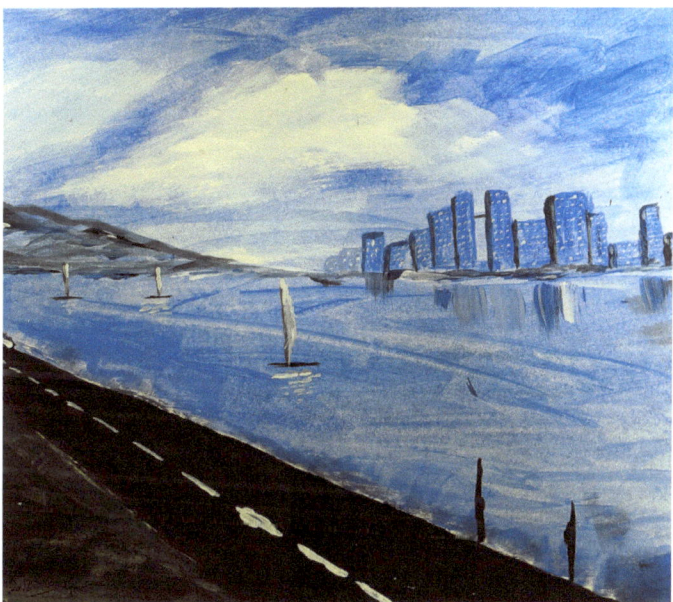

UNTITLED (SUNSET WITH BRIDGE), 2016, Abdualmalik Abud, paper, pigment, dimensions TBD

Held by Erin Thompson in New York City

The bridge in this work bears a resemblance to San Francisco's Golden Gate Bridge, but, as happens with many American icons featured in detainees' artwork, the landmark is illocatable and contexless. Abdulmalik said he did not have access to television or lms at the time of this work's creation.

UNTITLED (CITYSCAPE), 2016, Abdualmalik Abud, paper, pigment, dimensions TBD

Held by Erin Thompson in New York City

The work features an inviting skyline of buildings the color of sea and sky, but they are unreachable from the determined- seeming road in the foreground.

AMMAR AL-BALUCHI

Ammar Al-Baluchi, originally from Kuwait, was held by the CIA for three and a half years before arriving at Guantánamo, where he has been a "high value detainee" for ten years. He is currently held at Guantánamo's Camp 7, where security is even tighter than at the main camp. There, art-making is not officially sanctioned and detainees have only sporadic access to art supplies. The simple existence of this work is remarkable.

Ironically, while Al-Baluchi has little ability to make art of his own, he is another artist's (unwilling) subject: a character named "Ammar," who is shown being tortured in the 2012 film Zero Dark Thirty is based on information about Al-Baluchi given by the CIA to the filmmakers, but not to him or his lawyers.

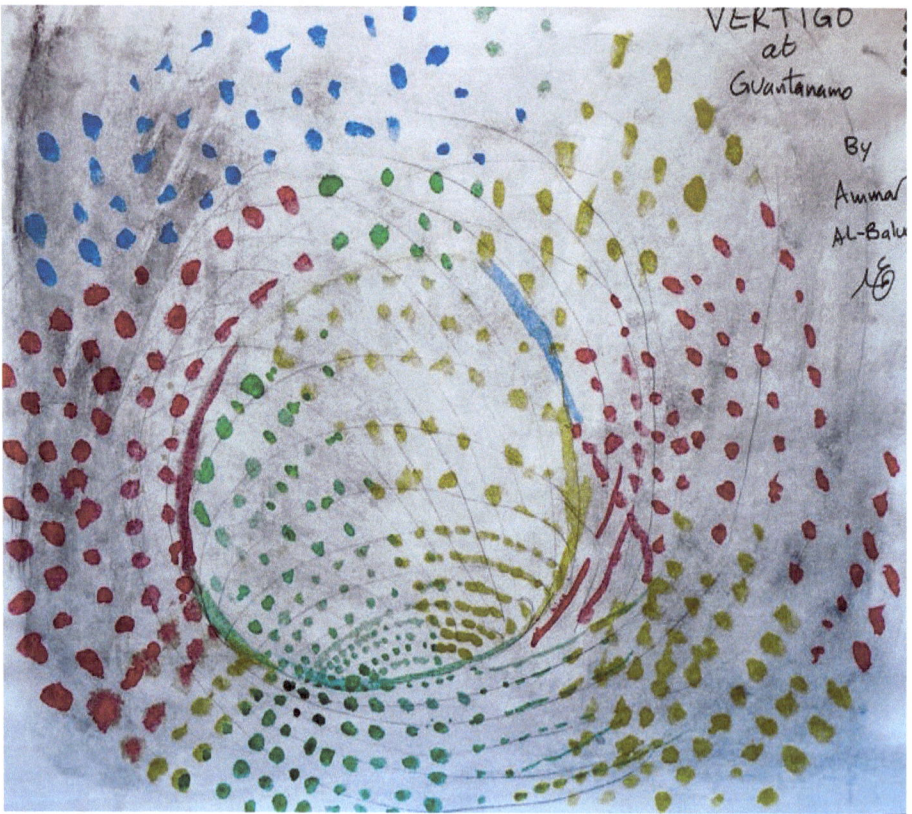

VERTIGO AT GUANTÁNAMOA, 2016, Ammar Al-Baluchi, Paper, graphite, watercolors, 9 x 12

In the collection of Alka Pradhan

Al-Baluchi made this work in an effort to explain to his lawyers the vertigo he suffers after he sustained a traumatic brain injury during interrogation.

AHMED RAHBBANI

Ahmed Rabbani, a citizen of Pakistan, has been held at Guantánamo for nearly 13 years. Detained and tortured by the CIA before arriving at Guantánamo, Rabbani has protested by undertaking years-long hunger strikes, resulting in daily violent force-feeding. Pain lies just under the surface of many works by Rabbani, who signs his paintings with his nickname, Badr.

UNTITLED (BINOCULARS POINTING AT THE MOON, 2016, Ahmed Rabbani, Paper, pigment, 18 x 20 in

held by Beth D. Jacob in New York City

Asked by his lawyers to explain his artwork, Rabbani wrote in Arabic on the back of this painting:

Huge Moon. Everyone in meteorology anticipated and followed this event. And I, infatuated, passionately anticipated seeing this strange event where the moon was at its closest point to earth since 70 years ago.

Initially, this appears to be a simple memento of the Super Moon, a much-reported cosmic event in November 2016. However it is difficult to ignore Rabbani's parallels with the moon: the countless unseen eyes at the end of binoculars seem to represent the authorities who have scrutinized every aspect of Rabbani's life without, as he claims, understanding it at all.

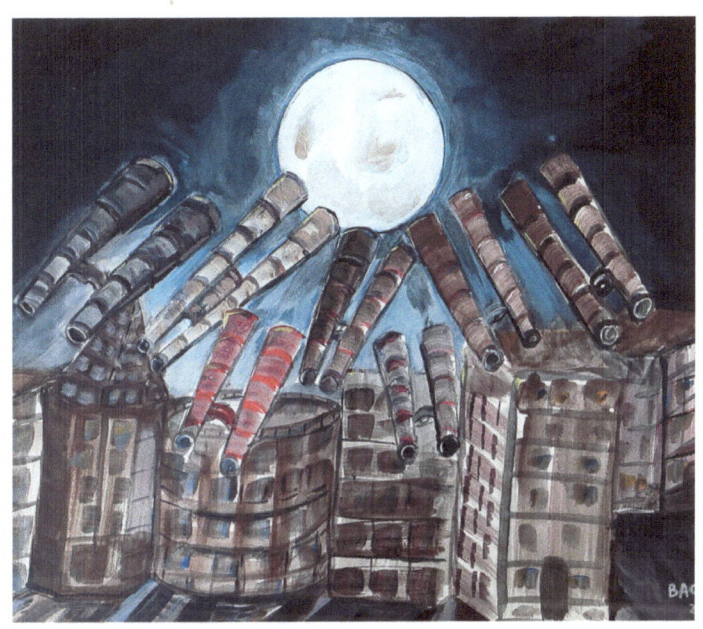

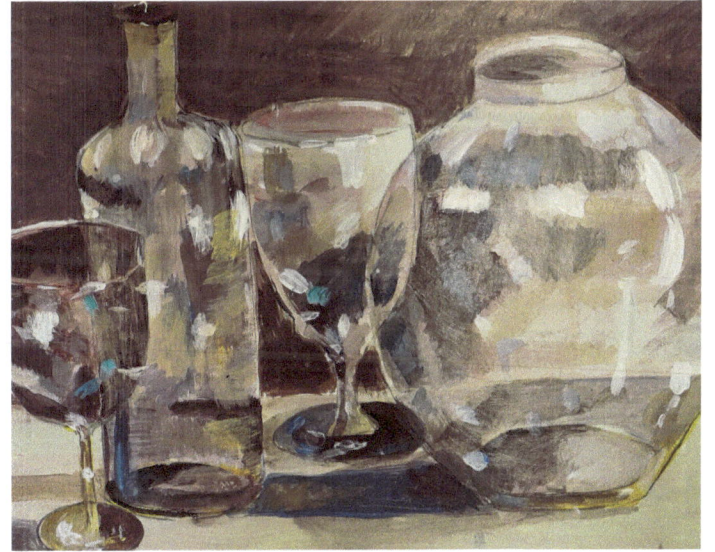

UNTITLED (STILL LIFE OF GLASSWARE), 2015, Ahmed Rabbani, Paper, pigment, 9 x 12 in

held by Reprive US in New York City

Upon first glance, this work appears to be the result of a still life assignment that could have been given in any painting class. But the empty vessels also serve as an oblique reference both to Rabbani's absent family and to his acts of self-denial and resistance.

DJAMEL AMEZIANE

DJAMEL AMEZIANE WAS BORN IN ALGERIA BUT FLED AS A REFUGEE. HE ARRIVED AT GUANTÁNAMO IN 2002. ALTHOUGH HE WAS CLEARED FOR RELEASE IN 2008, HE WAS HELD FOR FIVE MORE YEARS, DURING WHICH TIME HE CREATED MOST OF HIS ART. HIS LAWYERS FOUGHT AGAINST HIM BEING RETURNED TO ALGERIA, BUT HE WAS EVENTUALLY TRANSFERRED THERE IN 2013.

UNTITLED (SHIPWRECKED BOAT), 2016, Djamel Ameziane, Watercolor (original), 20 x 25 in

framed inkjet scan held by Center for Constitutional Rights (CCR); original owned by the artist's brother in Canada

UNTITLED (BUILDINGS ON A SHORE), 2016, Djamel Ameziane Watercolor, 15.5 x 19

original (watercolor) held by CCR, framed inkjet scan owned by artist's brother

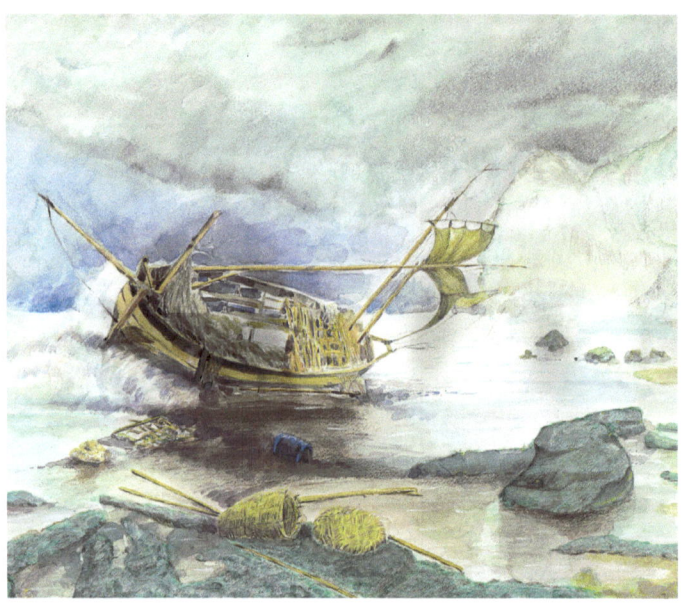

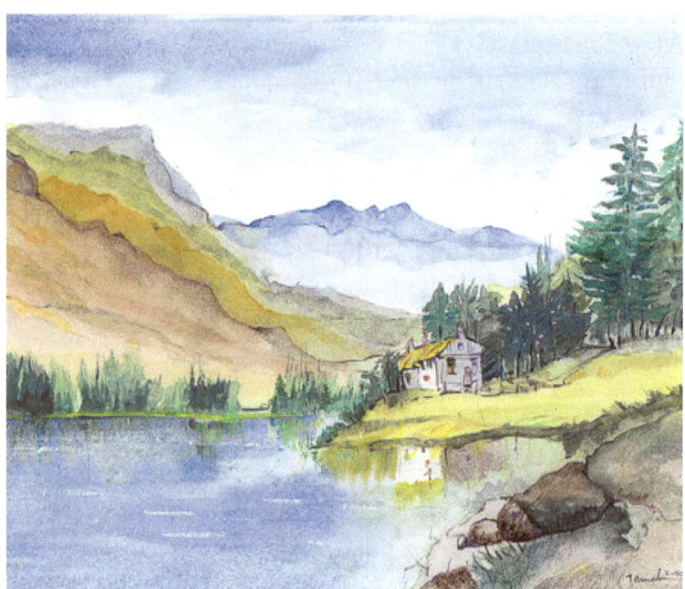

Ameziane told his lawyers that at his "worst moment" he felt as though he were "a boat out at sea, battered by successive storms during its trip towards an unknown destination...."

This watercolor of a shipwreck with no survivors reflects Ameziane's anxiety about his future at the time of its creation.

GHALEB AL-BIHANI

Ghaleb Al-Bihani, a Yemeni citizen, was detained at Guantánamo for nearly 15 years before being released to Oman in January 2017. Ghaleb, who discovered a talent for art in routine classes offered to detainees, once wrote, "Painting makes me feel as if I am embracing the universe....I also see things around me as if they were paintings, which gives me the sense of a beautiful life." Most of his paintings and drawings were created after 2014, when he was cleared for release, and sometimes depict his musings on what his life would look like when that release finally came.

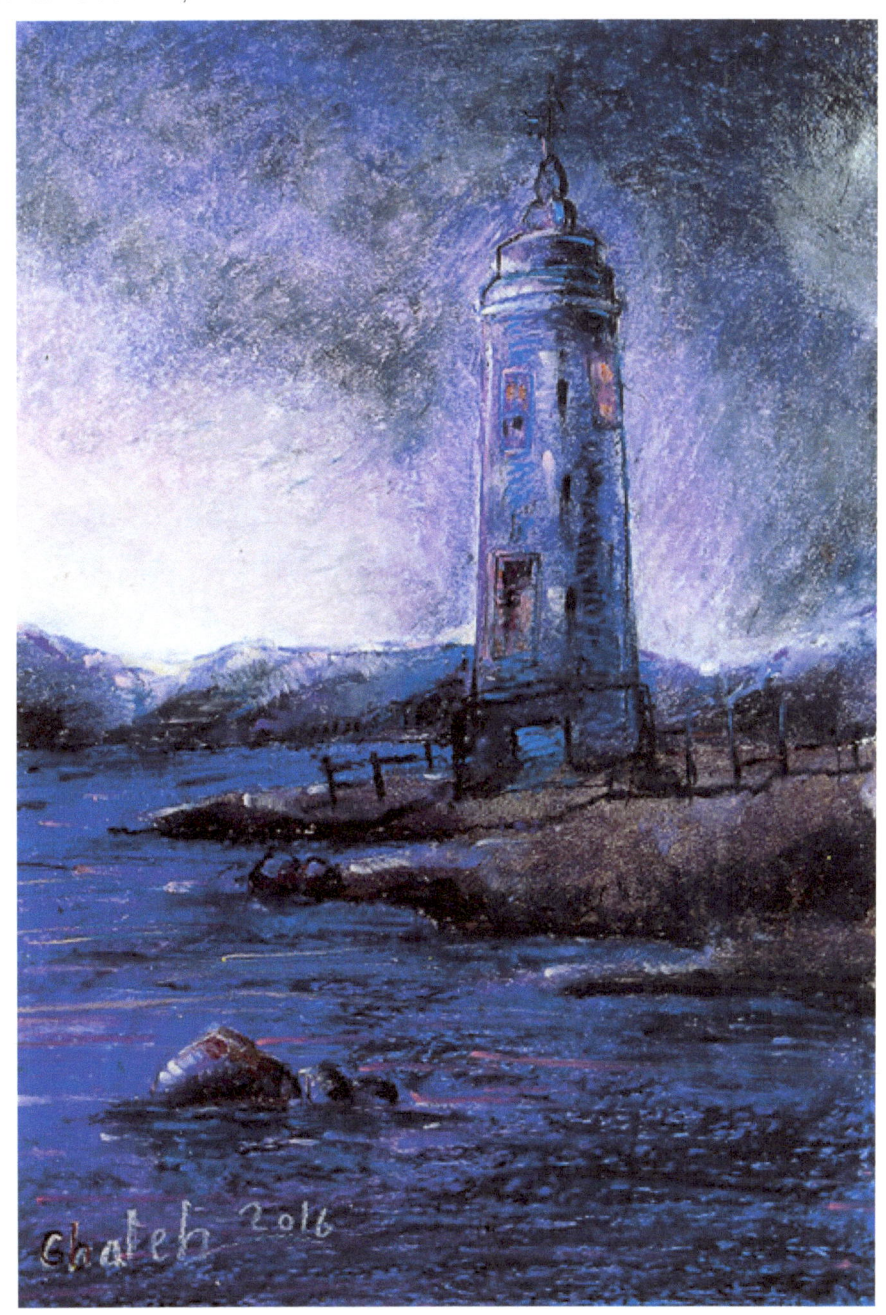

UNTITLED (LIGHTHOUSE), 2016, Ghaleb Al-Bihani, Paper, oil, pastels, 17 x 11.5 in

The warning beacon on on this brooding lighthouse has been extinguished.

UNTITLED (RED AND PURPLE BOAT)G2015, Ghaleb Al-Bihani, Paper, oil, pastels, 12 x 9 in
held by CCR
Empty boats are a common subject in the detainees' art. Although empty, these boats are unmoored, as if they are carrying invisible portraits of the artists.

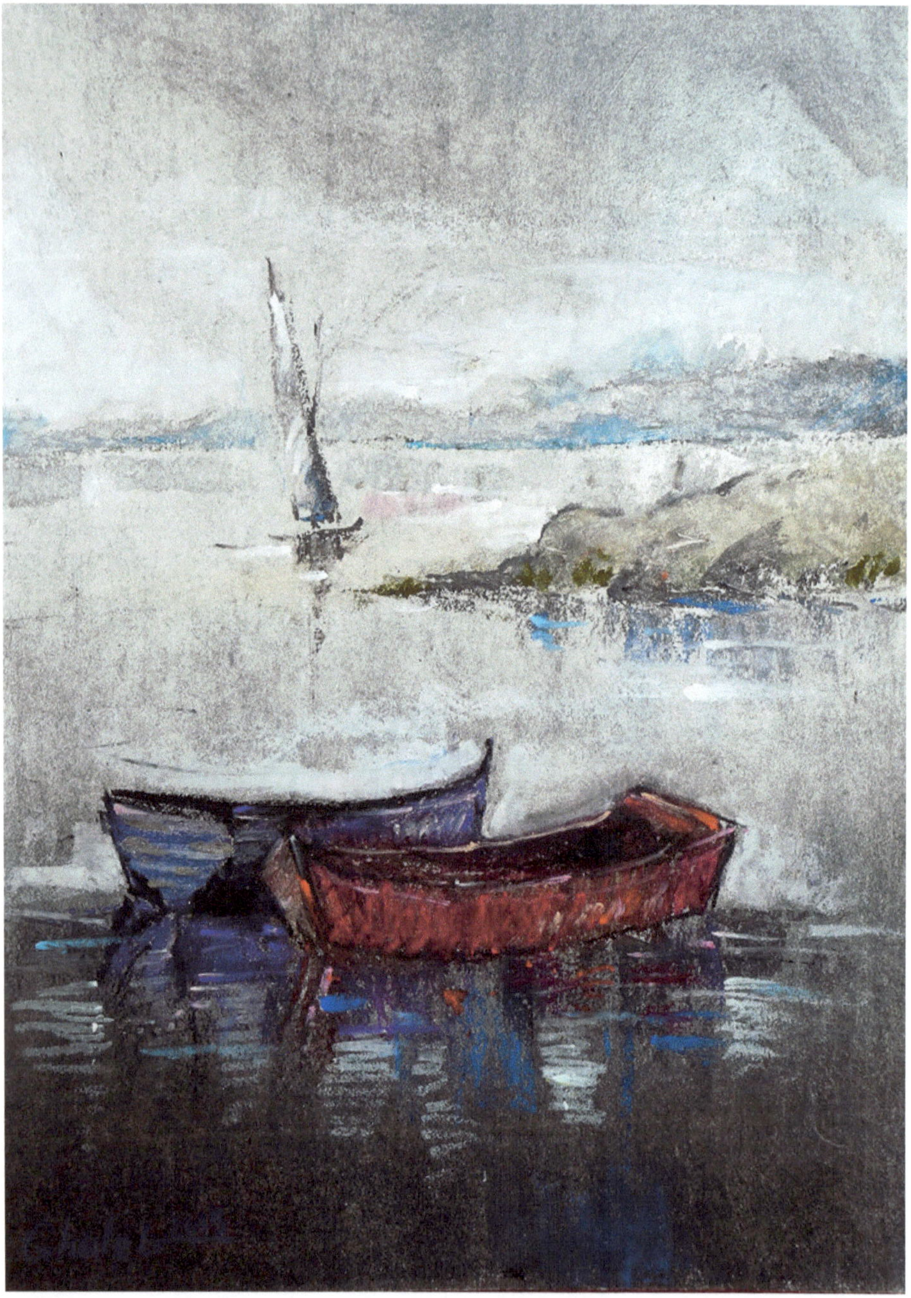

UNTITLED (HANDS HOLDING HEART WITH RIBBON), 2016, Ghaleb Al-Bihani, Paper, pigment, 25 x 20 in,

held by CCR

The rounded, delicate nature of these arms and hands suggest that they belong to a woman. In the detainees' art, hearts often symbolize members of the artists' family. Al-Bihani told his laywers that he tried to imagine what his future wife would be like, if he was able to marry after his release. Perhaps this work shows that imagined woman, cradling a heart draped in fabric that is both a decorative ribbon, and a bandage.

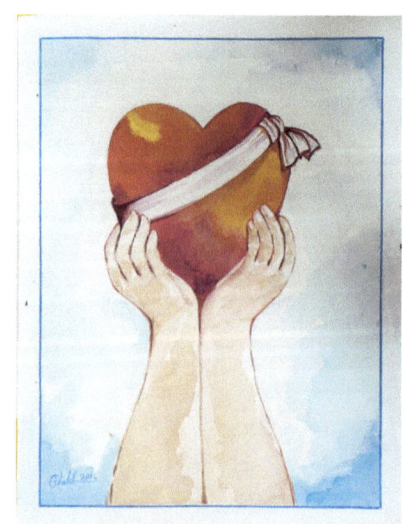

UNTITLED (BLUE MOSQUE), 2016, Ghaleb Al-Bihani, Watercolor, 18 x 23.5 in

held by CCR

After initial years of tight control of media, detainees are now allowed greater latitude in what they can consume. At first there were no televisions, then one, then many, with satellite TV stations, leading detainees to incorporate images from current events into their artwork.

After a 2016 terrorist attack on Istanbul's Blue Mosque, Al-Bihani created this work as a gestrue of solidarity with the victims there. The lush and idyllic landsape in which Al-Bihani places the Mosque demonstrates the often optimistic way in which detainees combine images from various sources of locales they cannot visit.

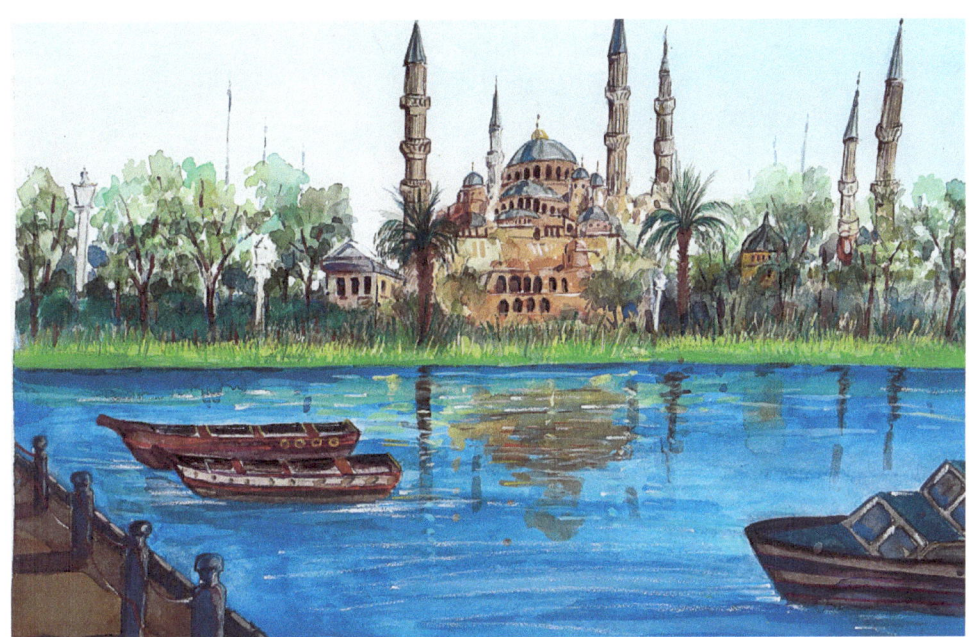

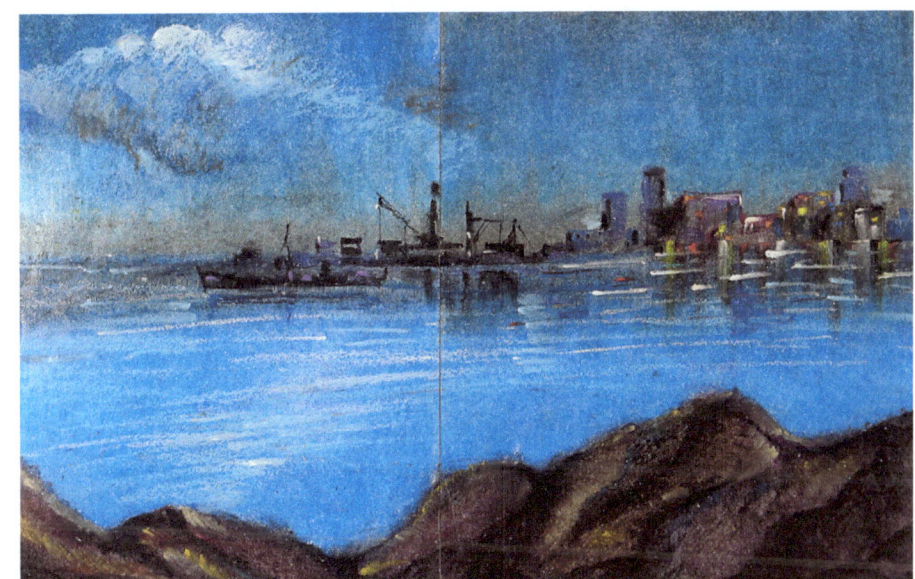

UNTITLED (LARGE SHIP AGAINST A SKYLINE), 2015, Ghaleb Al-Bihani, Paper, pigment, 12 x 18 in

held by CCR

Al-Bihani depicts a bustling city, separated from his viewpoint by mountains and water.

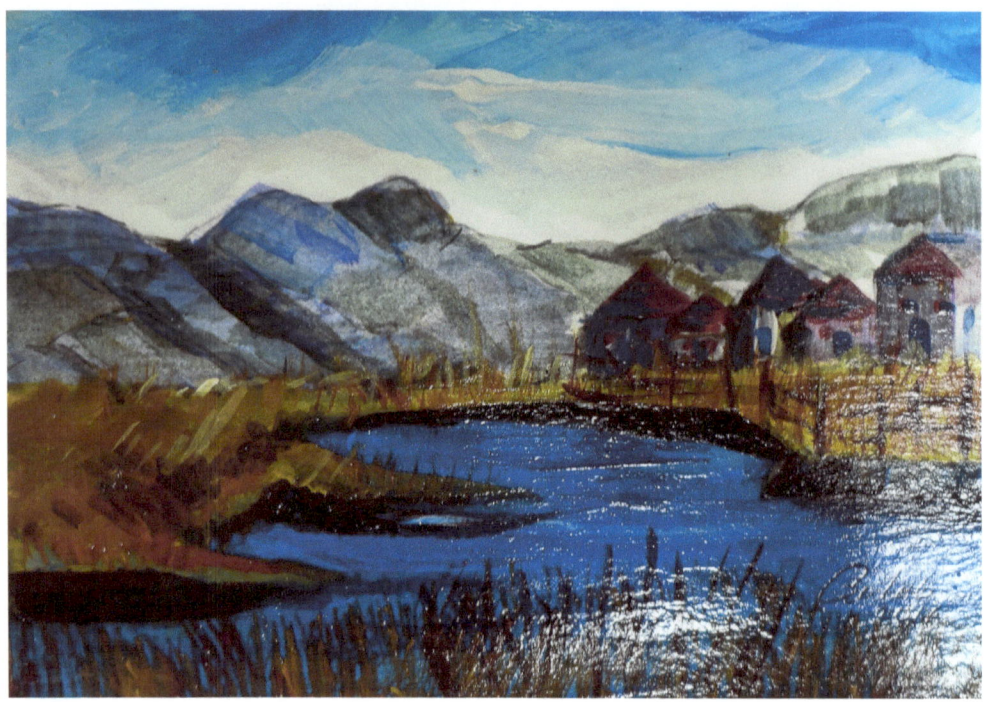

UNTITLED (HOUSES REFLECTED IN A BAY), 2015, Ghaleb Al-Bihani, Paper, pigment, 9 x 12 in

held by CCR

There are very few human figures in the artwork that has been permitted to leave Guantánamo. Many branches of Islam forbid creating figurative artwork of humans. Although not all of the detainees are especially religious, it is possible that artists chose subject matter knowing the inclusion of people could prevent more fundamentalist detainees from enjoying their work. It is also possible that paintings containing human figures are much more likely to be used as evidence against detainees when facing review for release. Regardless of why, the paintings in this exhibition are largely desolate, leaving the viewer to interpret the faint suggestion of humanity in each scene, including the uninhabited houses seen here.

UNTITLED (TWO PALMS),
2016, Ghaleb Al-Bihani, Paper, pigment, 5 x 3.5 in

held by CCR

Al-Bihani created this small painting with an audience outside of Guantánamo in mind. He knew that his representatives at the Center for Constitutional Rights often distribute materials at public events, so he made an image suitable for printing as a postcard, hoping to contribute to his own advocacy.

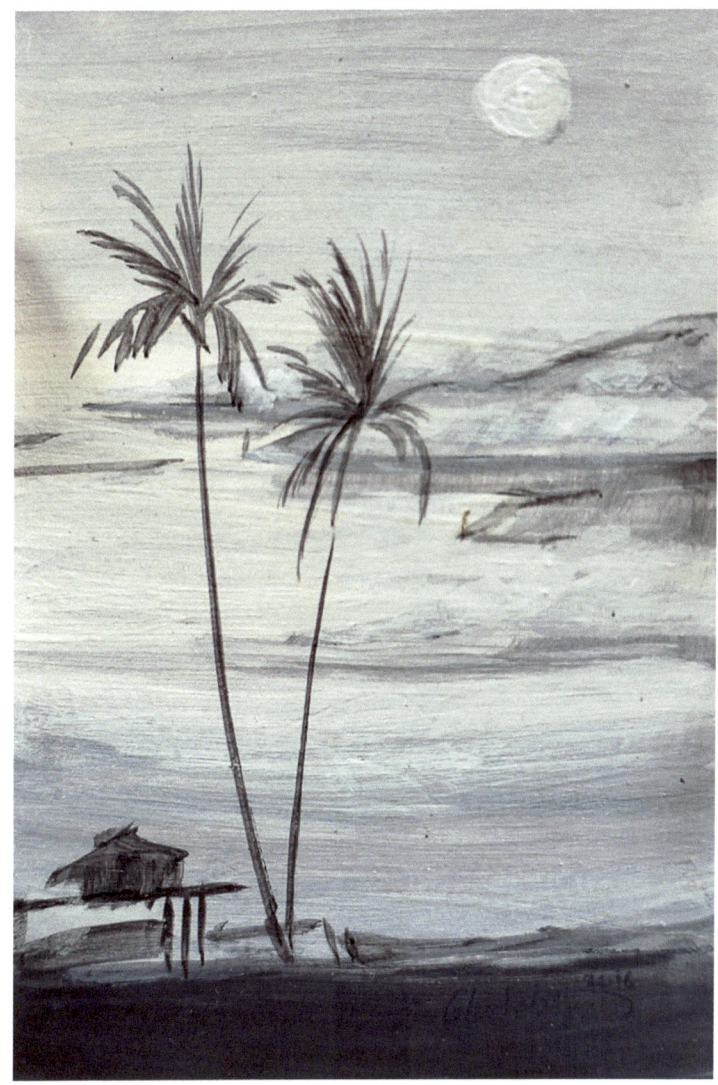

KHALID QASIM

Khalid Qasim, originally from Yemen, has been detained at Guantánamo for over 15 years. He signs his works with his work with his prisoner number, 242.

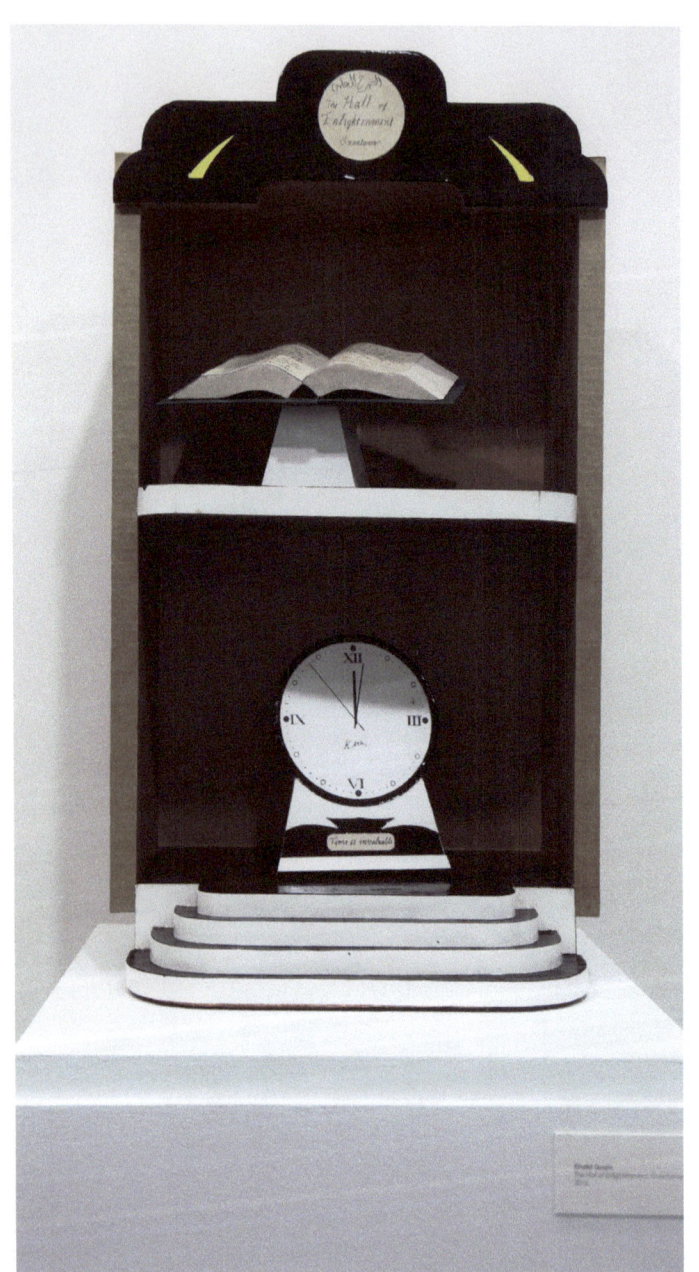

THE HALL OF ENLIGHTENMENT, GUANTÁNAMO, 2016, Khalid Qasim, meals ready to eat boxes; paint (coffee grounds mixed wih glue); various found and mixed media, 30 x 17 x 4 in

held by Reprive US in New York City

The book's carefully-lettered inscription reads,

As represented by the stairs, the only way to establishing a strong foundation of knowledge is by one step at a time. As depicted by the clock, time is an essential element therefore every moment must be cherished. One must not wait to acquire knowledge as time has already begun ticking. The flat top indicating the infinity of knowledge—the more you attain, the more you desire. 1:30 AM Fri Sep. 9, 2016, K 242, Guantánamo, Cuba.

This text is as a guide for interpreting his work: a meditation on the quest for self actualization by an artist whose most basic future is uncertain.

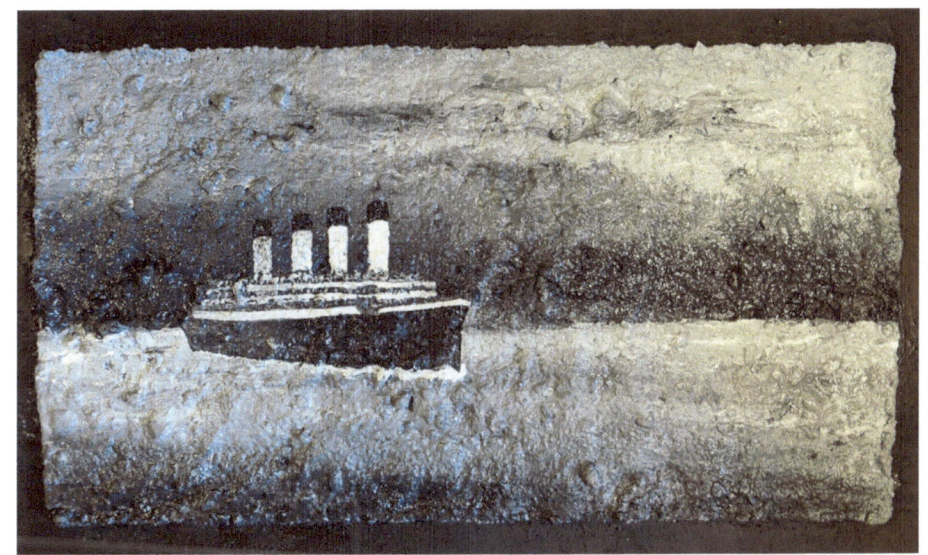

UNTITLED (TITANIC), 2017, Khalid Qasim, cardboard; gravel, sand, rock (collected from the prisoners' exercise yard) mixed with glue; paint, 10 x 16.5 x .6 in
2017

held by Reprive US in New York City

UNTITLED (FINS IN THE OCEAN), 2016, Khalid Qasim, Paper, paint, 14 x 17 in

held by Reprive US in New York City

Many works in this exhibition that depict seascapes. This piece shows, perhaps most explicitly, the anxieties and fears lying under the surface of seemingly tranquil waters.

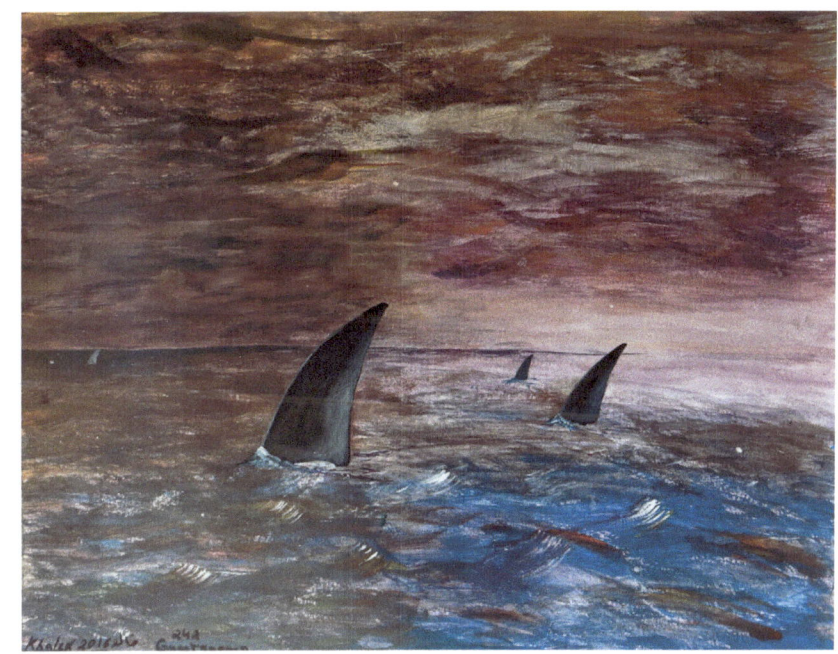

MOATH AL-ALWI

MOATH AL-ALWI HAS BEEN HELD AT GUANTÁNAMO SINCE 2002. NOT SATISFIED WITH THE LIMITED ART SUPPLIES PERMITTED TO DETAINEES, HE SEEKS OUT OTHER MATERIALS TO CREATE HIS ELABORATE MODEL SHIPS, INCLUDING CARDBOARD, OLD T-SHIRTS STIFFENED WITH GLUE, AND BOTTLECAPS.

WHILE WORKING ON THESE VESSELS, AL-ALWI TOLD HIS LAWYERS HE IMAGINES HIMSELF IN THE MIDDLE OF THE OCEAN.

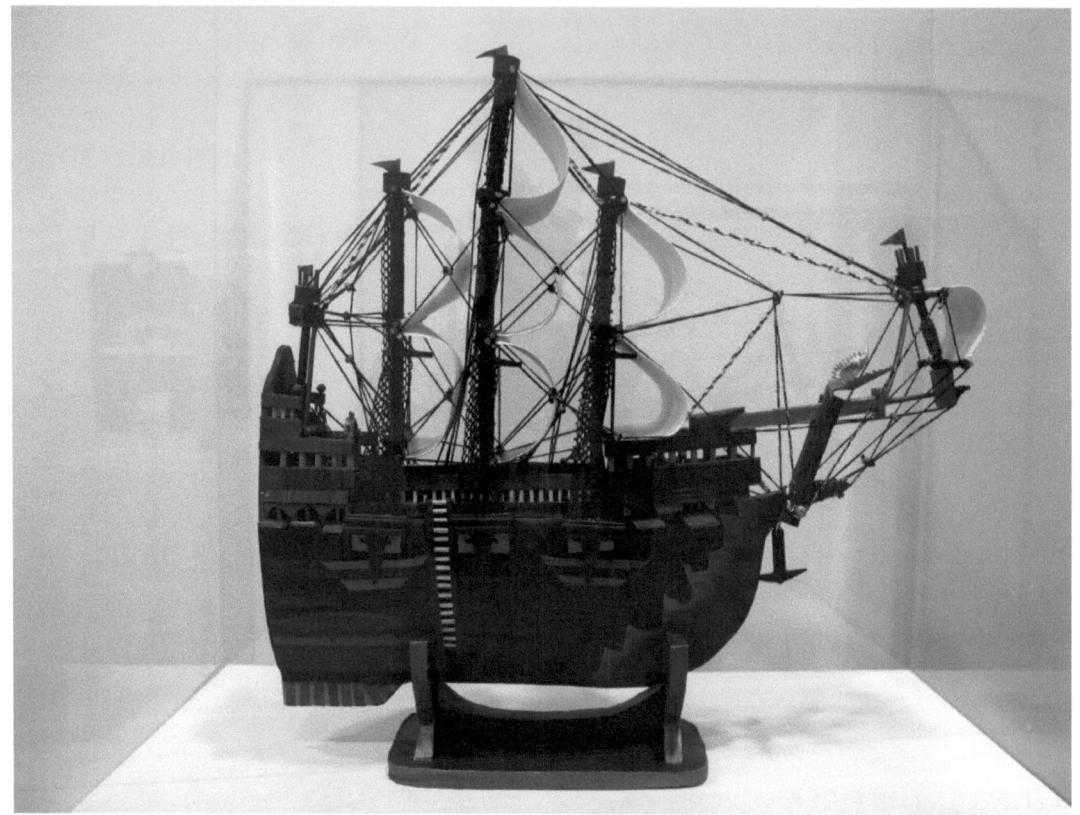

UNTITLED (MODEL SHIP), 2015, Moath Al-Alwi, assemblage ; mixed media; sculpture, 26 x 26 x 7 in

held by Beth D. Jacob, to be gifted to his family at the exhibition's conclusion.

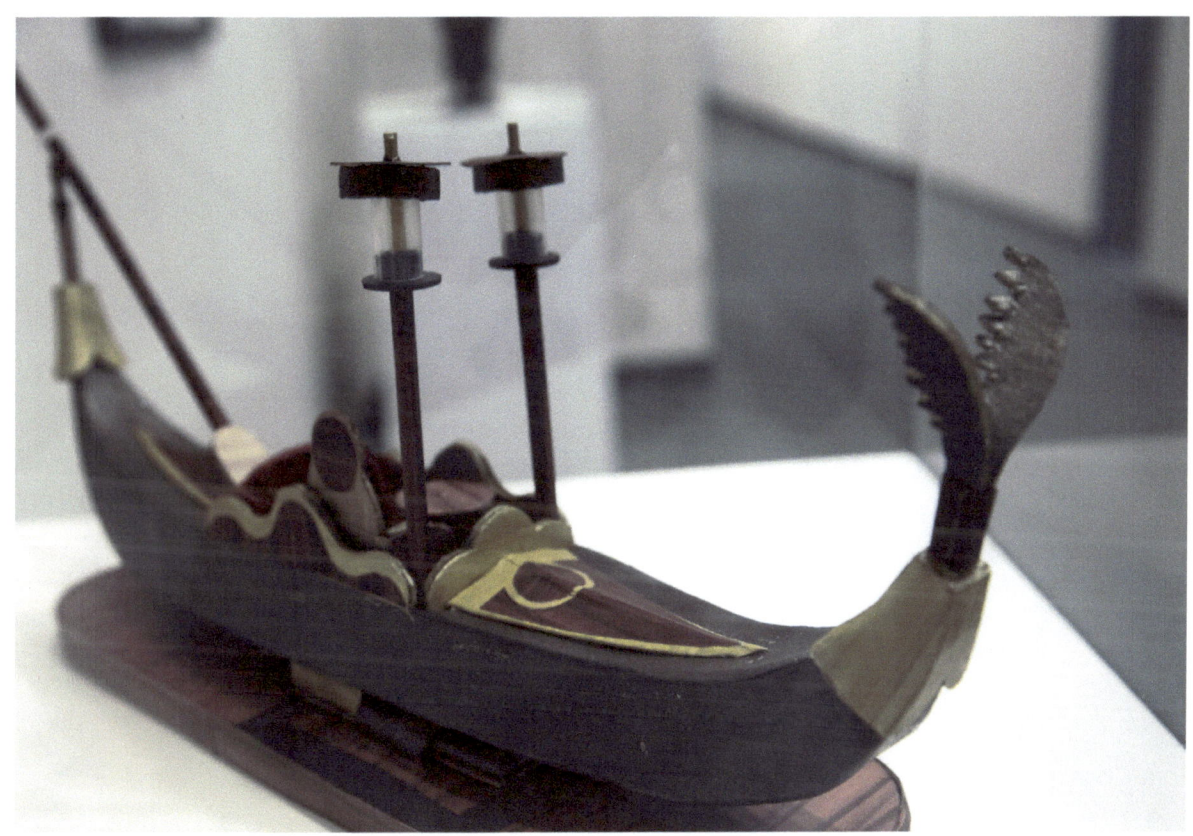

UNTITLED (MODEL GONDOLA), 2016, Moath Al-Alwi, 12 x 8 x 4 in, assemblage ; mixed media; sculpture

gifted to Beth D. Jacob

The glass of the lanterns on this work are made from the plastic covers of razors Al-Alwi is given for shaving.

MUHAMMAD ANSI

Muhammad Ansi, originally from Yemen, was transferred to Oman in January 2017 after being detained at Guantánamo for almost 15 years.

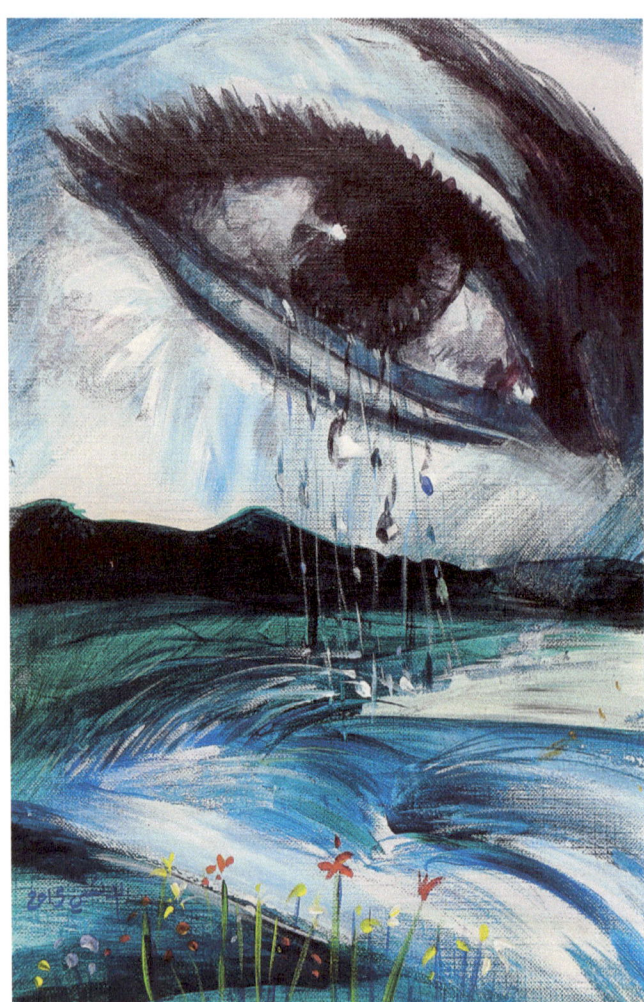

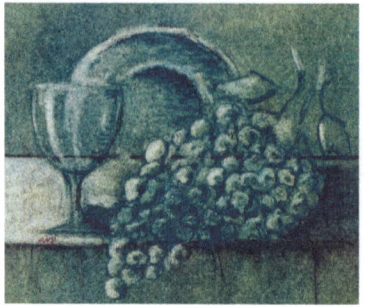

UNTITLED (STILL LIFE IN GREEN) M2016, Muhammad Ansi, Paper, oil, pastel, 9 x 12 in

held by Beth D. Jacob in New York City

Some of the detainees' works look like the art exercises produced by students anywhere–but they were made by men shackled to the floor of the art classroom.

UNTITLED (PIER), 2016, Muhammad Ansi, Paper, pigment, 12 x 18 in

held by Beth D. Jacob in New York City

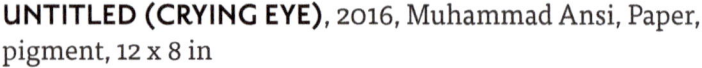

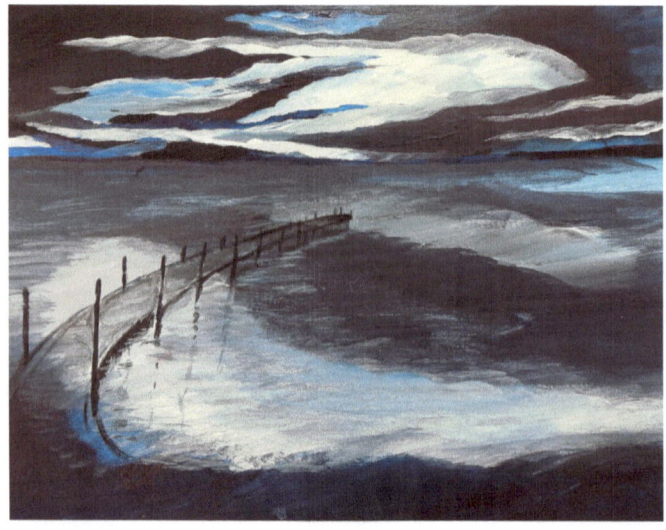

UNTITLED (CRYING EYE), 2016, Muhammad Ansi, Paper, pigment, 12 x 8 in

held by Beth D. Jacob in New York City

After the Periodic Review Board initially denied Ansi's application for release, his works showed the tension between expressing his pain and repressing emotions that the Board would see as a negative in future hearings. Only to his lawyer did Ansi eventually reveal that this crying eye represents his mother.

UNTITLED (WINGED HEART), 2016, Muhammad Ansi, Paper, pigment,

held by Beth D. Jacob in New York City

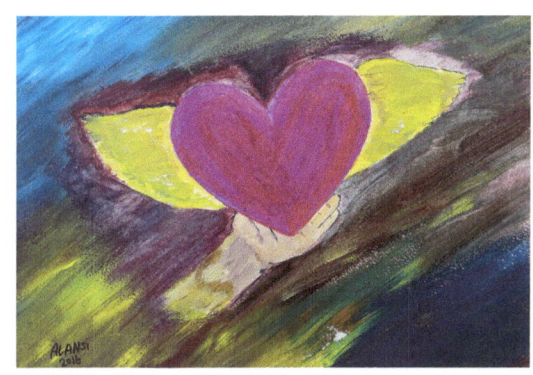

UNTITLED (SUNBATHERS), 2016, Muhammad Ansi, Paper, pigment, 18 x 12 in

held by Beth D. Jacob in New York City

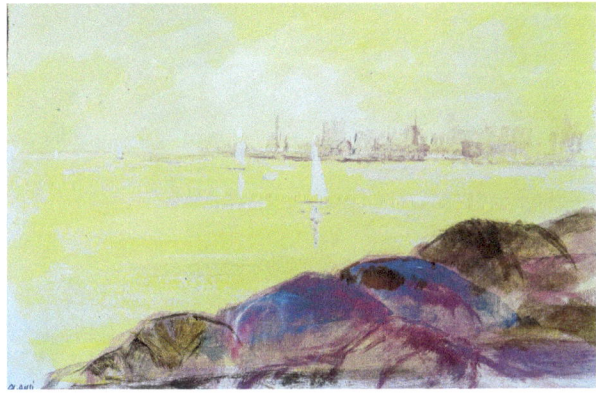

UNTITLED (SAILBOATS IN YELLOWS),2016, Muhammad Ansi, Paper, pigment, 9 x 12 in

held by Beth D. Jacob in New York City

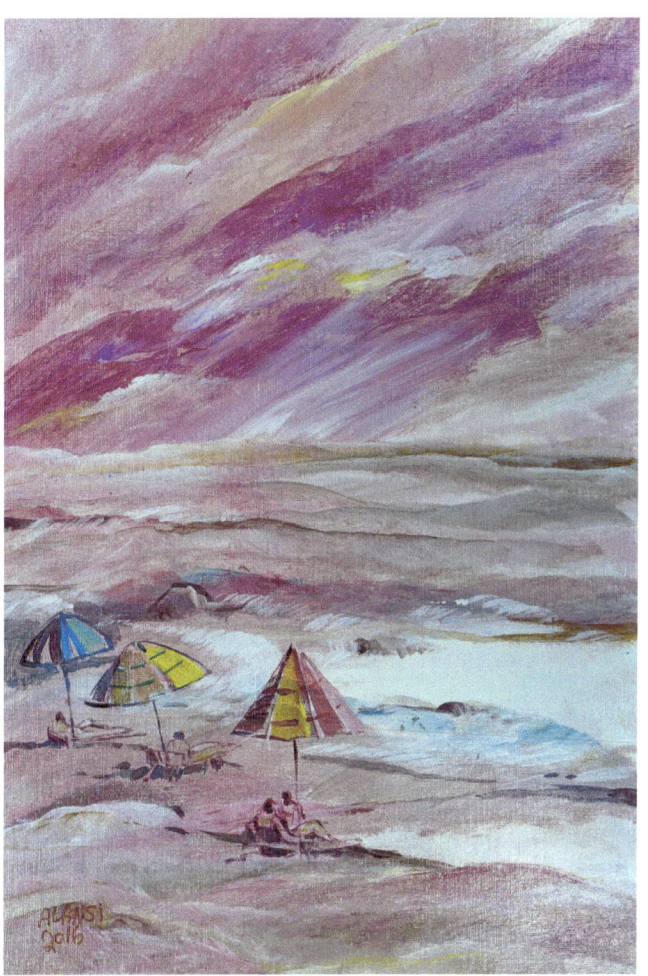

UNTITLED (TITANIC), 2016, Muhammad Ansi, Paper, pigment, 18 x 24 in

held by Beth D. Jacob in New York City

This painting recalls the trauma of interrogation. When Ansi's interrogators changed their tactics from force to trying to create rapport with him, they used a female interrogator. In her first session, she and Ansi watched the 1997 Hollywood blockbuster *Titanic*—the first movie Ansi had seen. Ansi recalls this viewing with mixed emotions: he was entranced by the film, but recognized the attempted manipulation of being shown sexual scenes while sitting beside a woman.

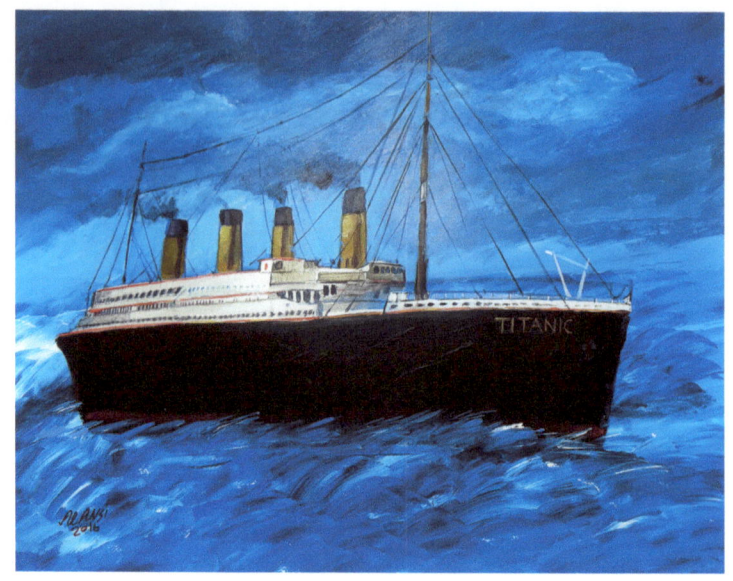

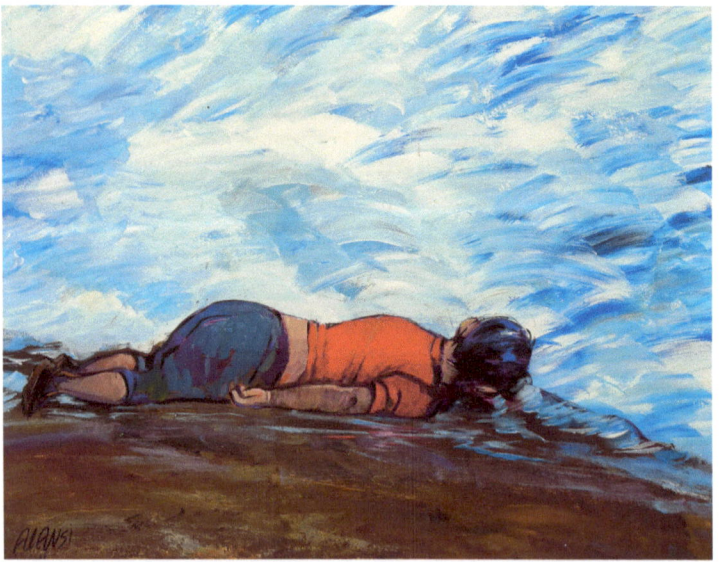

UNTITLED (ALAN KURDI), 2016, Muhammad Ansi, Paper, pigment, 22 x 28 in

held by Beth D. Jacob in New York City

This work is Ansi's reproduction of a photograph of Alan Kurdi, a refugee child who drowned while fleeing conflict in Syria. The photograph was reproduced endlessly in 2016, but Ansi refocuses the attention on the individual, human tragedies of war. His painting stands as witness: this death is such that it should be mourned even by someone whose own life has been destroyed by war.

UNTITLED (HANDS HOLDING FLOWERS THROUGH BARS), 2016, Paper, pigment, Muhammad Ansi, 11 x 8.5 in

held by Beth D. Jacob in New York City

Ansi painted a pair of hands clutching the bars of a high window—only later did he add flowers, inserting their stems in the fists. The hands are simultaneously yearning for escape and making a peace offering to the world outside the cage. The work, upon closer inspection, captures the faint pencil marks recording Ansi's first impulse: he sketched hands whose fingertips barely reach above the window opening, grasping desperately, like those of a man drowning in the middle of the sea.

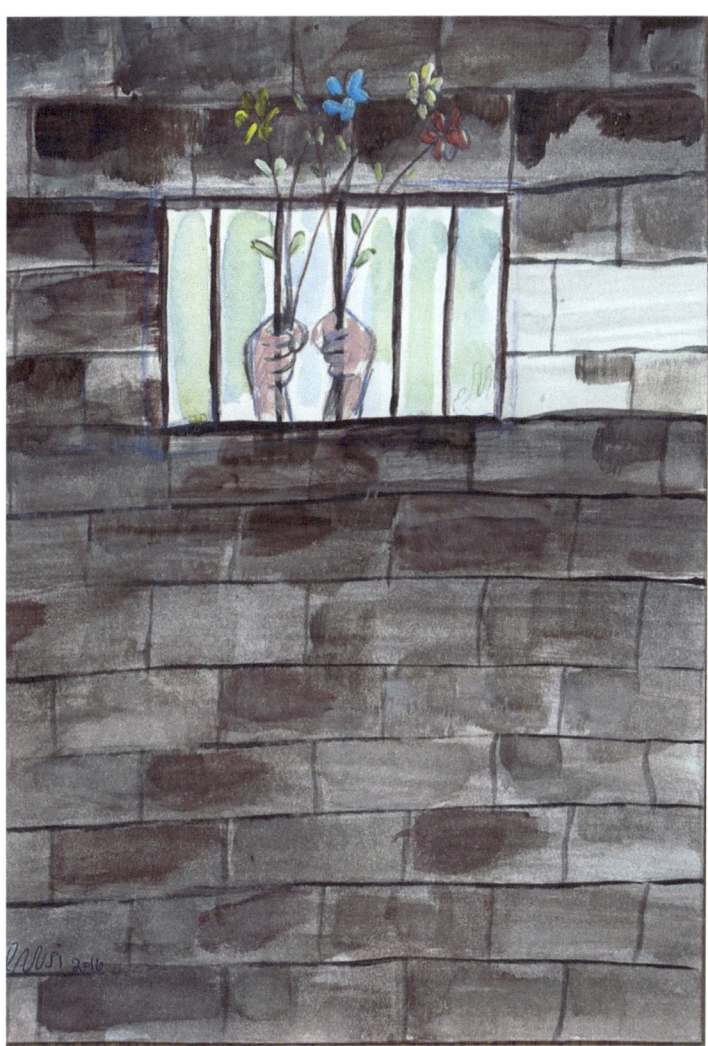

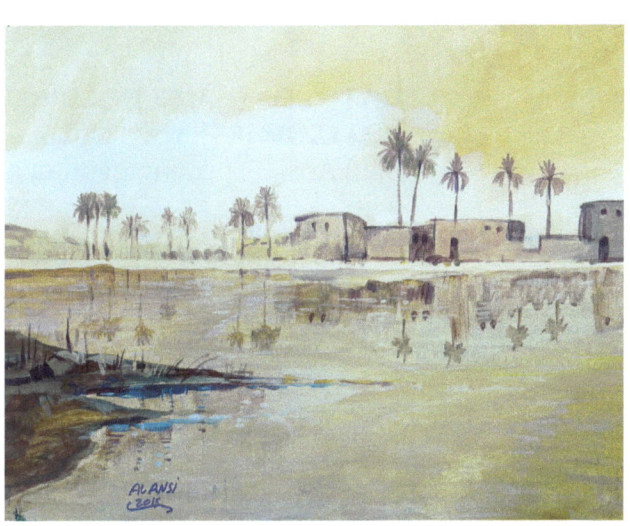

UNTITLED (OASIS), 2016, Muhammad Ansi, Paper, pigment, 9 x 12 in

held by Beth D. Jacob in New York City

Many of the seascapes in this show, when not completely unlocatable, contain vaguely western imagery. This piece may refer to a locale closer to Ansi's home.

UNTITLED (STORM AT SEA), 2016, Muhammad Ansi, Paper, pigment, 8 x 12 in

held by Beth D. Jacob in New York City

The materials given to detainees are all soft: pens, pencils, and pallet knives are generally forbidden. Despite these limitations, Ansi achieves a sharply poignant scene with furious brushstrokes where it is difficult to distinguish between the sea and the ship it is devouring.

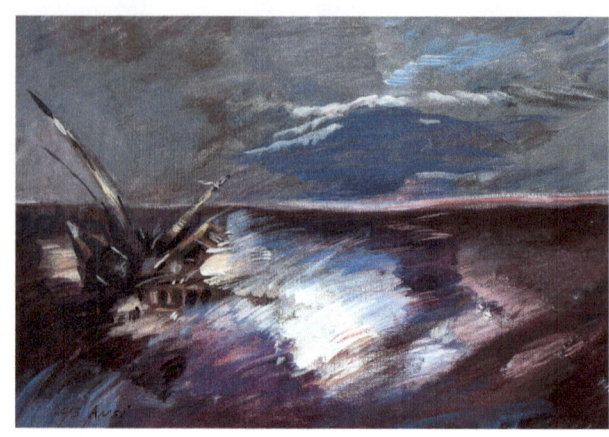

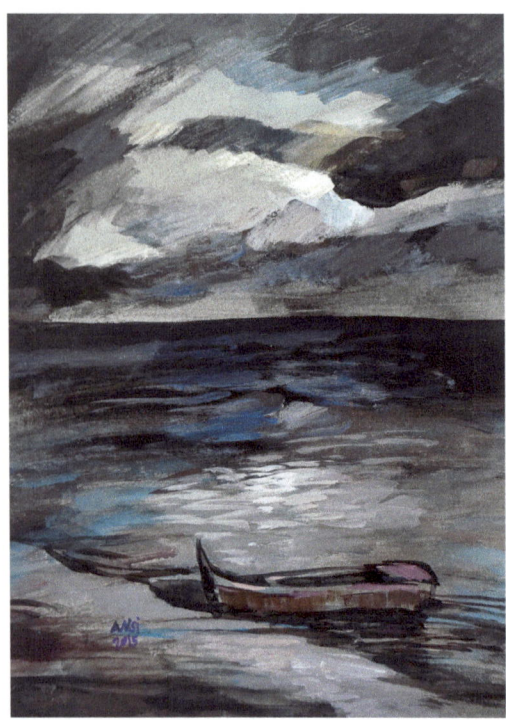

UNTITLED (BLACK SHORE), 2016, Muhammad Ansi, Paper, pigment, 8.5 x 11

held by Beth D. Jacob in New York City

A coffin-like boat washes up on a shore under black skies.

UNTITLED (HAND HOLDING RED FLOWERS), 2015, Muhammad Ansi, Paper, pigment, 12 x 9 in

held by Beth D. Jacob in New York City

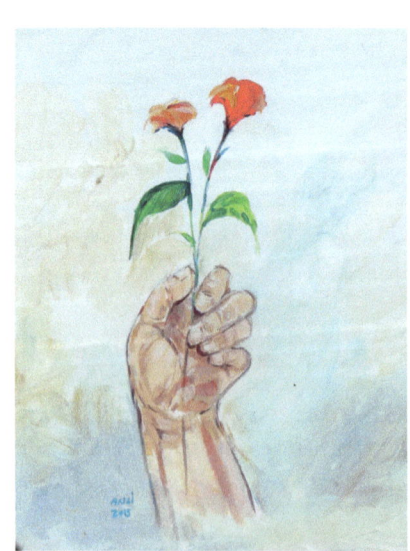

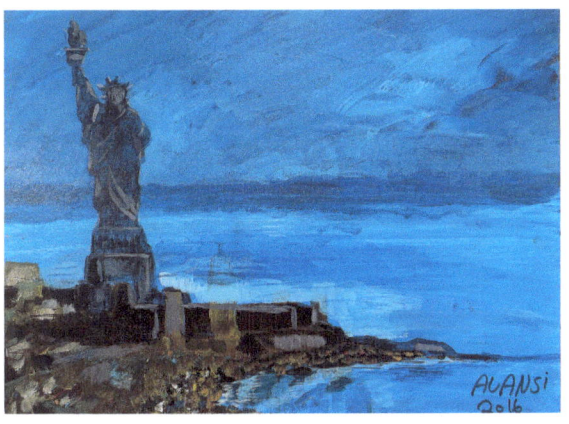

UNTITLED (STATUE OF LIBERTY), 2016, Muhammad Ansi, Paper, pigment, 8.5 x 11

held by Beth D. Jacob in New York City

Because the guards at Guantánamo are American, almost all of the detainees have a functional knowledge of American culture. Despite the fact that none of the detainees are permitted to enter America, the Statue of Liberty appears in their works. Here, Ansi paints her in shades of black, presiding over a desert island, with a background that might be the New York City Skyline, but might only be banks of clouds.

UNTITLED (STATUE OF LIBERTY), 2016, Muhammad Ansi, Paper, pigment, 8.5 x 11

held by Beth D. Jacob in New York City

Because the guards at Guantánamo are American, almost all of the detainees have a functional knowledge of American culture. Despite the fact that none of the detainees are permitted to enter America, the Statue of Liberty appears in their works. Here, Ansi paints her in shades of black, presiding over a desert island, with a background that might be the New York City Skyline, but might only be banks of clouds.

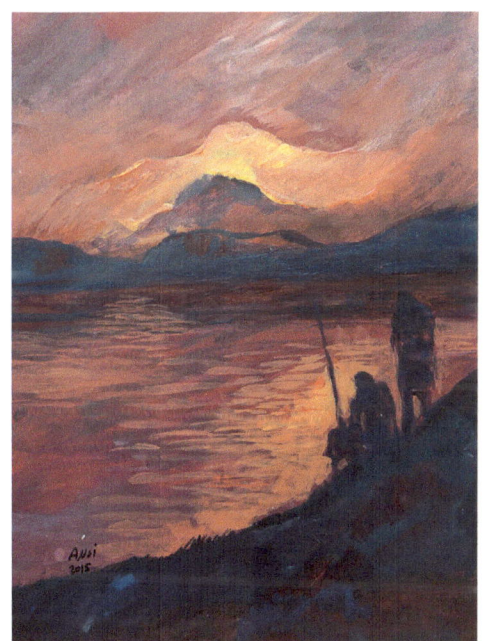

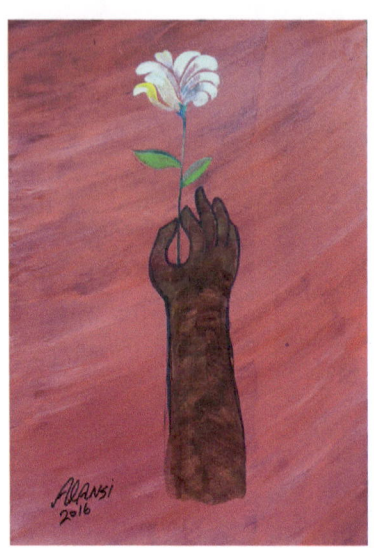

UNTITLED (HAND HOLDING A FLOWER), 2016, Muhammad Ansi, Paper, pigment, 17

held by Beth D. Jacob in New York City

There are instances of several detainees painting the same subject multiple times with multiple variations. While some tableaus, such as glassware or grapes, seem to be reasonably standard images provided by an art class instructor, other repeated subjects, such as this hand holding a flower, might speak to detainees taking lessons from each other.

LETTER, *from* MUHAMMAD ANSI
to NYC *artist*

My Best Greetings,

Thank you very much for your beautiful letter. I was extremely happy with it because it is the first letter I have ever received from an esteemed artist like you. The thing that honored me most is the term "Your Friend." I was happy to read this term which made me stop and think about it for a whole day. I cannot but say that I had forgotten this term. I have not heard it in the last fifteen years.

Just to let you know, most of the art materials and techniques you mentioned in your letter, this is the first time I have heard about them. Here, we have very limited means to do what we do, but still they achieve the purpose. I even don't dare to say my "art work," I usually call them my colored papers.

I love nature because it is the most beautiful thing in the universe. Nature generously gives its beauty to all humans, animals, and all without any discrimination based on religious affiliation, language or country. She gives her air, water, skies, sun, moon and colors to all. I wish from the bottom of my heart to be like her, loving all with no view to any differences.

Your Friend,

Muhammad al Ansi

This letter has been edited and condensed by Erin Thompson.

POSTPRINT MAGAZINE

EDITOR-IN-CHIEF,
ETC. CHARLES SHIELDS

THANK YOU

Erin Thompson, Paige Laino,

the Center for Constitutional Rights, Reprieve US, Alka Pradhan of the Military Commissions Defense Organization, Beth D. Jacob, Suprita Datta, Gail Rothschild, Ran Kampel, Julian A. Jimarez Howard, Melaney Portillo, Amanda King

IN THE CURATION OF

ODE TO THE SEA: ART FROM GUANTANAMO

October 2, 2017 to January 26, 2018

President's Gallery
John Jay College of Criminal Justice
New York, NY

ISBN 978-0-692-99686-7